EV

IS

AN EINSTEIN;
AND THERE
IS
AN EINSTEIN
IN EVERYONE

The Constitution of Genius

by

BENJAMIN MICHAEL

PRODIGY PARADIGM PRESS

Prodigy Paradigm Press
Lanham, MD 20706

Ordering Information:
For details, contact Benjamin.Michael264@gmail.com

Library of Congress Control Number: 2020914243

Print ISBN: 978-1-09832-949-5
eBook ISBN: 978-1-09832-950-1

Cover design by Jelena Mirkovic
Front cover photograph © iStock by Getty Images™
Back cover photograph © iStock by Getty Images™

Typesetting by Arrow Graphics, Inc.
www.arrow1.com

Printed in the United States of America on SFI Certified paper

To
the
Loving
Memory
of
My
Dear Mother

Contents

References
·139·

Acknowledgements
·143·

Index
·145·

A Note from the Author

I was infused with inspiration after listening to the unabridged audio version of *Outliers: The Story of Success* authored by Malcolm Gladwell. Press fast forward a few years and after also reading the books *Out of Our Minds: Learning to be Creative* and *The Element: How Finding Your Passion Changes Everything*, authored by Sir Ken Robinson. I was convinced I had an array of ideas that, collectively, could knit together a timely written book. The core of the book would build on the aforementioned work done by Mr. Gladwell and Mr. Robinson and dredge a new pathway of thinking. That is the origin that gave rise to *Everyone is an Einstein; and There is an Einstein in Everyone: The Constitution of Genius*. As you read from cover to cover, consider the material through the lens of your own personal experiences. Take the time to see parallels to the personal experiences of your spouse, your children, your family, your friends and coworkers. The stories and examples are much more like your story and mine than you may believe at first glance.

—BENJAMIN MICHAEL

PREAMBLE

"genius"

"TO RAISE NEW QUESTIONS, NEW
POSSIBILITIES, TO REGARD OLD PROBLEMS
FROM A NEW ANGLE, REQUIRES CREATIVE
IMAGINATION...."

—ALBERT EINSTEIN

As a collective human culture, we continually strive to *reimagine* and *redefine ourselves* to more fully and accurately *imagine* and *define ourselves*. Time and time again, what have we done when we have found that previously held ideas, concepts, theorems, and, yes, definitions have become inadequate and antiquated in some instances? We have self-corrected them with more thoughtful, more nuanced, more comprehensive ideas, concepts, theorems, and definitions. If asked to name a "genius," who is the first person that springs to mind? Walter Isaacson provided the following introduction to one of our more famous *geniuses* (if not the most famous):

> Their first child was born at 11:30 a.m. on Friday, March 14, 1879, in Ulm, which had recently joined, along with the rest of Swabia, the new German Reich.

1

Initially, Pauline and Hermann had planned to name the boy Abraham, after his paternal grandfather. But they came to feel, he later said, that the name sounded "too Jewish." So they kept the initial A and named him Albert Einstein.

The name of Isaacson's book is *Einstein* and it provides a very detailed account of Einstein's life. In many people's mind, Albert Einstein is the quintessential "genius", and the man credited for "the world's most famous equation," $E = mc^2$. My question for you is, collectively, as human beings, does the mind of Albert Einstein embody the paradigm that we use when defining genius?

It is common knowledge that Einstein had a prodigious and very illustrious career. The awards he won, the tributes named after him are many, and here a just a few:

2008: Einstein was inducted into the New Jersey Hall of Fame.

1999: *Time* magazine named Einstein the person of the Century.

1979: The Albert Einstein Memorial in Washington, D.C. is a bronze statue depicting Einstein seated with manuscript papers in hand.

1953: The Albert Einstein College of Medicine is located in the Morris Park neighborhood of the Bronx in New York City.

1955: Einsteinium (Es) is a synthetic chemical element (atomic number 99) named after Einstein.

1935: Einstein was awarded the Franklin Institute's Franklin Medal for his extensive work on relativity and the photo-electric effect.

1929: Einstein presented with the Max Planck medal of the German Physical Society for extraordinary achievements in theoretical physics.

1925: The Royal Society awarded Einstein the Copley Medal.

1921: Einstein awarded the Nobel Prize in Physics.

I find it interesting how the word "genius" is used in our collective cultural vocabulary. Often times the word genius is used in very abstract terms; to the degree that the term genius is sometimes couched during conversations and through the pages of books, magazines, and literature in a manner that excludes, vice framed from an inclusive perspective. In a manner that excludes from the perspective one may receive the impression that the "genius" referenced is some sort of superhuman celestial being, whose talents or accomplishments are vastly beyond anything that you and I would ever be able to achieve through our own efforts and initiative. The geniuses of the past and present are not an elite/chosen few; geniuses do not solely originate from certain privileged classes of societies; geniuses are not only nurtured and groomed within the confines of a select few dominant cultures; and geniuses are not only innately spawned by a certain race. I think it's vitally important to restate the aforementioned common knowledge in order to reinforce the underpinning of this book: Each of us is a *Genius*. Furthermore, *Everyone is an Einstein; and There is an Einstein in Everyone.* Ask someone that you know or even a stranger the following question: Do you consider yourself a genius? It's very likely that you'll find many who respond "no." My question back to them is by whose definition are they not a *Genius?*

Merriam-Webster gives multiple definitions of genius:

ge·nius *noun* \\'jēn-yəs, 'jē-nē-əs\\

1—extraordinary intellectual power especially as manifested in creative activity

2—a person endowed with transcendent mental superiority

3—an extraordinary, undeniable, unique, adaptable, elastic, and non-stationary-force that (1) resides in every human being from birth and (2) is continually developed throughout life

Definition three encapsulates my definition of *Genius* and is the perspective from which this book is written. While I understand the vantage points from which the first two definitions of genius are written, we should not be handcuffed or limited by the understanding and parameters they provide. For the sake of differentiation, I will use a capital "G" (i.e., Genius) to identify my definition of Genius and a lower-case "g" to identify the general, commonly understood definitions of genius. My definition of *Genius* identifies, in very clear terms, the fact that it *"(1) resides in every human being from birth and (2) [it] is continually developed throughout life."* The *"extraordinary, undeniable, unique, adaptable, elastic, and non-stationary-force"* referenced in my definition encompasses, though is not limited to, the following mosaic of factors: the initial familial culture and other cultures and subcultures that build our language—that shape our approach and our way of thinking, and contours our way of understanding ourselves and the world around us; the intangible unique prism through which we individually receive, view, analyze, and interpret our experiences throughout life; the lessons we learn, the social, behavioral and intellectual habits and propensities we develop through the adversities, triumphs and day-to-day *jungle* gyms throughout life; and educational tools and resources (e.g., *self*, peers, parents, siblings, teachers, mentors, books, technology) used to continuously chisel, mold, refine our cognitive (mental processing) and intellectual (ability to reason) faculties and physical bodies throughout life.

There is not anything mystical in a supernatural sense about people who exhibit genius or people who exhibit *Genius*, although, the extraordinary range of creativity, imagination, innovation, and/or physical mastery that spawn from *Genius* or genius may at times, on the surface, appear supernatural. My definition underscores that Genius is not an abstract state of being, only discovered and exhibited by a privileged or lucky few. Antithetically, *Genius* is incubated within the innermost recesses of every child at birth and is continuously evolving *(non-stationary-force)*, adapting *(adaptable)*, and stretching *(elastic)* in a practical sense, being formed and shaped during every microsecond of our lives.

The prism through which we cognitively experience (mental processing) life and make sense of those experiences (intellect/ability to reason/ability to control our physical body) is quite *unique* to our person. Every human being has unique fingerprints. Similar to the nature of the human *fingerprint*, the *Genius* within each of us is invariably unique. In Albert Einstein's case, we've seen in his numerous findings, accomplishments and achievements, the dimensions, scope, and breadth of his *fingerprints* on the study of Physics. What social, political and/or scientific problem, economic theory and/or economic solution, or technological creation and/or technological innovation do your *fingerprints* advance and/or solve? What insights and depth of enlightenment do your *fingerprints* provide? What do your *fingerprints* look like through the lens of your *passion*, and what unique perspective do your *fingerprints* offer? In other words, *fingerprints* in the following sense:

Fingerprints (manifestation of your Genius) = *the specifics of your unique scientific postulate; the formula of your unique mathematical algorithm; the code specific to your unique software program; the unique thought pathway to your unique invention; the notes to your unique musical composition; the epiphany associated with your unique philosophy; the artistry exhibited in your unique theatrical performance; the range and timbre of your unique voice; the clarity of thought, precision, and grace associated with your unique writing style; the enlightenment that reverberates from your unique polemic epistle; the revelation induced from your unique way of delivering a sermon; the style, dexterity, and form associated with* *your unique athletic ability; the unique conciseness of facts when off the teleprompter and command delivered through your words during your news telecast and/or news report, and on and on.*

The unique "fingerprints" and Genius of Ari Melber, an American attorney and journalist, and Stephen "Steve" Schmidt, an American communications and public affairs strategist, come to mind. Ari is the *intellectually agile, nimble host* of *The Beat with Ari Melber* on the cable news channel MSNBC (still as of May 2020). Steve routinely offers his *uniquely wide-ranging, incisive political analysis* as if delivered more so with the razor-sharp blade of a surgical scalpel than with a human tongue. These are two brief examples of practical real world "fingerprint" manifestations of Genius. Again, I can go on and on.

Our respective uniqueness, our respective unique *Genius,* our respective unique fingerprints are universal attributes we should spotlight, highlight and celebrate openly and often; innate attributes to be honed, sharpened and recognized in each of us. Our respective Genius is portable and can be applied to those subject areas we choose. Regardless of the subject area or arena (e.g., Math, Science, Track & Field, Technology, Music, Politics, Journalism, the Arts), cause, vocation, or career of choice, Genius exists within each of us to cultivate talents, contributions, and achievements the world has never seen, as expressed through our *unique fingerprints.* In our human culture, we tend to speak about people who have strived and achieved extraordinary accomplishments in far more favorable light subsequent to their death. Conversely, in some cases, we fail to recognize, appreciate, and properly value the gifts, talents, and unique *Genius* of many people while they are still alive. Regardless of the level of recognition, spotlight, notoriety, or lack thereof, we may receive during the course of our lives or after, each unique fingerprint counts.

Develop into a *technician* in how your fingerprint *technique* manifests your Genius. Many of us have observed and experienced the fingerprints, the technique of well-known and not so well-known technicians, so to speak. Over the years, we've learned about and witnessed the manifestation of fingerprints originating from the likes of Andrew M. Cuomo (Governor/Leadership), George Will (Journalism), Barbara Walters, Rachel Maddow, Ted Kopple, and Tom Brokaw (Television or Broadcast Journalism), Doris Kearns Goodwin and Jon Meacham (Historian), T.D. Jakes (Pastor), Adele and Sade Adu (Music), President Barack Obama and President Abraham Lincoln (Politics), Adam Schiff (Politics), Albert Einstein (Physics), Cornell Brooks (Activist), Bob Costas, Doris Burke, and Marv Albert (Sports Broadcasting), Amelia Earhart (Aviation), Michael Eric Dyson (Academic), George Lucas (Film), Oprah Winfrey (Television), Lin-Manuel Miranda (Theater), Leonardo da Vinci (Art), Jay-Z and Drake (Music), Roy Jones Jr. (Boxing), Gandhi (Civil Rights), Barry Sanders (Football), Vera Wang (Fashion), and Usain Bolt (Track and Field) to name a few. The size, reach, and scope of one's contribution to our society are not the only measures of significance and impact. The *famous names we know of* are simply the ones who have, through a collection of life events, penetrated their way into public life, pop culture, and/or history. You and I know of and have witnessed the manifestation of unique fingerprints of the not so well-known—our wives, husbands, children, nieces, nephews, grandparents, friends, neighbors—and their respective contributions to a wide spectrum of causes, sports, career fields, or vocations are also significant, also impactful.

Every so often we either read or hear a quote or excerpt from a book, whether originating from someone widely known or someone unknown that rivets the core of our soul in the most visceral way. The life-lesson, philosophy, or even the concept that the quote or excerpt encourages, discourages, or simply spotlights has a way of nailing, binding us to our seat or pinning us to where we stand. Consider the following excerpt from John C. Maxwell's book *Talent is Never Enough* against the backdrop of the unyielding desire to maximize human potential. What emotions and thoughts does the following excerpt engender in your heart and mind:

There's a story about a farm boy from Colorado[,] who loved to hike and rock climb. One day while climbing in the mountains, he found an eagle's nest with an egg in it. He took the egg from the nest, and when he got home, he put it under a hen along with her other eggs.

Since he hatched among chicks, the eagle thought he was a chicken. He learned chicken behavior from his "mother" and scratched in the chicken yard along with his "siblings." He didn't know any better. And when he sometimes felt strange stirrings within him, he didn't know what to do with them, so he ignored them or suppressed them. After all, if he was a chicken, he should behave like a chicken.

Then one day an eagle flew over the farm, and the chicken-yard eagle looked up and saw him. In that moment, he realized he wanted to be like that eagle. He wanted to fly high. He wanted to go to the mountain peaks he saw in the distance. He spread his wings, which were much larger and stronger than those of his siblings. Suddenly he understood that he was like that eagle. Though he had never flown before, he possessed the instinct and the capabilities. He spread his wings once more, and he flew, unsteadily at first, but then with greater power and control. As he soared and climbed, he knew he had finally discovered his true self.

Isn't each and every human being metaphorically an *Eagle*? Each human being is an Eagle in the sense that we are born with a uniquely human attribute of having the ability to soar, climb as far as our initiative and work ethic take us. Think reflectively about your own journey that has carried you to where you stand or sit today. Many times, because of extrinsic factors (e.g., lack of parental guidance, poverty, abuse, dilapidated schools, physical limitations and health conditions) and/or intrinsic factors (e.g., fear, doubt, lack of self-confidence), we may possess the toxic misperception that we are and were born *chickens*. Chickens in the sense that we may believe we are a different person other than an extraordinary unique Genius. For the record, I don't have any gripes with chickens in general; chicken was a dinner staple in my household growing up (author smiling). My point is that there are factors that can shroud our ability to see ourselves, to see our 'true selves,' as referenced in Mr. Maxwell's book, as clearly as we should—we may misperceive ourselves as *chickens*, instead of correctly understanding and properly perceiving ourselves as we were born; we were born *Eagles*. Regardless of your pedigree, regardless of how you look and where you come from, regardless of whether you had humble or generous beginnings, regardless of where you may find yourself today, *Eagles* we are. Let's deconstruct the excerpt and place it into perspective, juxtaposed against the backdrop of this book:

> Since he hatched among chicks, the eagle thought he was a chicken. He learned chicken behavior from his "mother" and scratched in the chicken yard along with his "siblings." He didn't know any better.

How often are we born in or find ourselves in adverse conditions, in struggling communities, and/or in turbulent circumstances that lead us to believe we are less capable, less extraordinary than we are in reality? We misbelieve that our condition, struggle and circumstance are who we are, instead of seeing ourselves clearly apart from them. Like the Eagle in the excerpt, often times we learn and ultimately adopt the cultural, social, behavioral, psychological, and intellectual habits of the environment we find ourselves in—it's important to note that this does not necessarily occur in every case, nor am I suggesting that it does. There are always exceptions to the norm, trailblazers, and pathfinders:

> And when he sometimes felt strange stirrings within him, he didn't know what to do with them, so he ignored them or suppressed them. After all, if he was a chicken, he should behave like a chicken.

In many instances, we have brief, ever so slight, glimpses or can see clearly through a massive window how truly exceptional we can become. Yet, because of where we find ourselves coupled with doubt and the misconceptions we have about ourselves as a result, we don't take the time to explore, discover, develop, and nurture our *passions* and *dreams*—we 'ignore them,' we 'suppress them,' or worse, we stifle them, until they wither away, having never taken the opportunity to grow them, cultivate them, and share them with the rest of our world:

> Then one day an eagle flew over the farm, and the chicken-yard eagle looked up and saw him. In that moment, he realized he wanted to be like that eagle. He wanted to fly high. He wanted to go to the mountain peaks he saw in the distance.

At some point in time, an epiphany occurs—we arrive at the realization that we are, in fact, as extraordinary as those brief glimpses we've seen and as exceptional as what we saw through the massive window of ourselves in our 'mind's eye.' We resolve to ourselves that we will not leave this earth until we maximize our innate, unique *Genius*, talents and abilities, as we endeavor to share our *passion* with the world. We decide it's not satisfactory to settle for less than the full realization of our potential. At this point, our minds ooze with brimming-ambition, relentless-determination, dogged-tenacity toward accomplishing our goals and objectives:

> He spread his wings, which were much larger and stronger than those of his siblings. Suddenly he understood

that he was like that eagle. Though he had never flown before, he possessed the instinct and the capabilities. He spread his wings once more, and he flew, unsteadily at first, but then with greater power and control. As he soared and climbed, he knew he had finally discovered his true self.

The beauty in this moment is when it states that "[h]e spread his wings [or unique *Genius* so to speak], which were larger and stronger than those of his siblings." At this juncture, we may realize that our unique *Genius* is equally, if not more effective, in some instances, than our peers or other so-called experts—more specifically, our talents and abilities may be more developed and better suited in some areas than those of our peers or so-called experts. Conversely, in practical terms, there may be areas where our talents and abilities may be less developed and not necessarily better suited in other areas than those of our peers or so-called experts. Based on where our *passion(s)* or *intrigue* lie and the depth to which we are motivated by that passion(s) or intrigue, the fact is that our development in certain areas correspondingly reflects the time and effort we've taken to harness the skill-sets associated with effectively performing the craft that is a consequence of that passion or intrigue. What is important is that we embrace our uniqueness in every regard. Furthermore, our minds are made up at this juncture, and we're willing to put everything on the line to fulfill our respective destinies. Risks don't scare us—the only risks that concern us are the risks of not unearthing the magnitude our true *Genius* and not plowing forward to reach our full potential. During the course of our journey, we rely on diligent study, careful preparation, deliberate practice, relentless repetition, and *humble* confidence to navigate, maneuver through obstacles and adversities that present themselves. You understand that *humility* is very important, considering that during the early stages of your journey, you are, in fact, a fledgling apprentice. You maintain your humility as you become more and more agile and nimble over time, with unique facility, dexterity, and acuity specific to your person, when performing the craft you are passionate about or intrigued by—you are an amazing sight to behold. You finally reach the point where you understand that although there is always room to improve, you are finally residing in the home of your passion; finally *living* in the *living room* of your dreams and not only *living in* your dreams—you "finally discover... [your] true self."

> There's a story about a farm boy from Colorado[,] who loved to hike and rock climb. One day while climbing in the mountains, he found an eagle's nest with an egg in it. He took the egg from the nest, and when he got home, he put it under a hen along with her other eggs.

The aspect that I appreciate about this segment is the reference to "eagle's nest." Although the eagle was removed from its nest and placed amongst chickens, the eagle's immediate condition, community, and circumstance ultimately did not change the fact that he (or she) is an *Eagle* and was born an Eagle. Equal to the example of the Eagle, as human beings, our immediate condition, community, and circumstance—which may be very humbling and gaunt—don't change the infinite potential that exits within each of us. We don't choose where we are born, nor the parents that born us. However, we have the opportunity to make choices subsequent to that event. I encourage you to find your passion, your intrigue, spread your wings, and fly, because you are emphatically an Eagle! Even if you fly clumsily, "unsteadily" at first, soar, climb, and share your unique *Genius* with our world through your sojourns, detours, and the remainder of your journey throughout life.

The human spirit in your fellow man can and will see the poetry and grace in your clumsiness and unsteadiness—the reason being is that when people see you, they can and will see themselves; they can and will see themselves in you, specifically, because you are them and they are you.

AMENDMENT I

Infinite Human Potential (Part 1)

"BETTER TO LIGHT A CANDLE THAN
CURSE THE DARKNESS."

—PETER BENENSON IN 1961

The Constitution of the United States is revered by its citizens, and its mettle has withstood the test of time. It is comprised of seven articles and twenty-seven amendments. Constitution Day is celebrated annually on September 17th, commemorating the formation and signing of the U.S. Constitution on September 17, 1787. Before the U.S. Constitution, the Articles of Confederation was the first written constitution of the United States. The Articles of Confederation, however, were weak with respect to its effectiveness, considering "the central government lacked the ability to levy taxes and regulate commerce...." The architecture of this book is closely aligned with the format of The Constitution of the United States, including a preamble and amendments. Constitution is defined as follows by Merriam-Webster.

con·sti·tu·tion *noun*| \ ˌkän(t)-stə-ˈtü-shən

1—the basic principles and laws of a nation, state, or social group that determine the powers and duties of the government and guarantee certain rights to the people in it

J.S. Mill wrote, "No great improvements in the lot of mankind are possible, until a great change takes place in the fundamental constitution of their modes of thought."

While there are no basic principles and laws enshrined in a formal constitution that govern how we bestow "genius" upon someone, the fundamental lens through which we view and understand the potential of every human being requires correction. By definition, an amendment seeks to correct something. Instead of chapters, I thought it appropriate to identify discrete sections of this book as *Amendments*, offering a more comprehensive and apt definition and understanding of *Genius*. The way we view and understand each other *influence* the way we approach and treat other. Under the umbrella of this new Constitution, the *new default* way we view and understand each other, the way we approach, esteem, and treat other, are totally upended. The myopic view that initially established someone like Ms. Misty Copeland as not having the right physique for ballet, despite her unique Genius for dance is antiquated. The shortsighted notion that to be considered a "genius" someone requires an IQ within range of Albert Einstein's no longer carries weight. From this point forward, every person born, every person we encounter is an Einstein, is a *Genius*. The "Genius" moniker is no longer reserved only for a select few. Any previous standards or criteria for genius that set apart Mr. Einstein, or any other persons similarly situated in terms of wide public acclaim or achievement like Einstein, from the rest of us are, again, antiquated. Regardless of IQ or perceived ability, Genius is inherent to every human being.

* * * *

It's very important to note I do not like movies; I LOVE movies and everything about the movie going experience. That includes the oversized movie screen, massive bag of Orville Redenbacher popcorn, the Butterfinger bites in a box, a healthy size container of pop, and maybe a box of Mike and Ike candies for good measure. Regardless of movie genre, simply said, I love movies. I love it all, from drama, art house films, comedy, to sci-fi, mystery, romance, fantasy, and the list goes on. I am a genuine movie buff, who appreciates the art of movie making and the artistry brought to life with performing/acting within a wide range of stories and storylines. Just as the artist Vincent van Gogh painted on canvases, so to do directors/production teams and actors create on the movie screen. I don't have the credentials of a Siskel & Ebert; I'm more so a humble dilettante in my expertise. A few all-time favorite actors of mine include the likes of Peter O'Toole, Cate Blanchette, Forest Whitaker, Thandie Newton, Joaquin Phoenix, and Michael Fassbender.

Every year when we hear the first person utter to their self, whether in a very low tone or high pitch voice, "Wow!!! The year has gone by in a blink of an eye—it's already Christmas-time," what movie, what movie title comes to mind? What movie title engenders the feel, the essence, the splendor of Christmas time!!? What timeless American movie classic instantly carries your imagination, heaves your senses into the uncontainable euphoria that generally revolves around Christmas time!!? The key word here is **Christmas-time**. Think... really think about it. Does it truly require a nanosecond for a movie title to float across your mind? If yes, take only one additional second to think. If you need more time, if you need more than one additional second, you may have missed out on one of the most exciting, priceless gems in a child's life; if you're a child who lived or lives in the United States that is. Needless to say, the answer is, or shall I say who can forget, the timeless American Christmas movie classic *It's a Wonderful Life* (1946).

In part, the next question continues to lead you into the destination and purpose of this book. Who can forget the performance given by James Stewart, who played the lead character named George Bailey? In my mind, his performance was unforgettable. That being said, as I steer you through my thoughts, pilot you through Amendments of this book, let's first remember and appreciate some of the numerous awards *It's a Wonderful Life* was nominated for and, in many cases, won:

Oscar (Academy Awards USA)

1947: Nominated for Best Actor in a Leading Role (James Stewart)

1947: Nominated for Best Director (Frank Capra)

Golden Globes, USA

1947: Won for Best Motion Picture Director National Board of Review, USA

1947: Won for Top Ten Films Cinema Writers Circle Awards, Spain

1949: Won CEC Award for Best Foreign Film National Film Preservation Board, USA

1990: Won National Film Registry Young Artist Awards

1994: Won for Former Child Star Lifetime Achievement

Who doesn't appreciate or who can't acknowledge the acting breadth and range James Stewart brought to the movie screen in *It's a Wonderful Life*—don't answer that! Personally, Stewart's performance in the movie *Rear Window (1954)* was also very memorable; another classic and favorite of mine.

Have you ever taken the time to analyze Stewart's performance to ascertain why it was so absolutely riveting, so absolutely mesmerizing in *It's a Wonderful Life*? I'm not a film critic, nor am I an expert when discussing the requisite attributes that are earmarks of a quality movie or what elements are essential for qualifying an individual performance as 'unforgettable' or 'Academy Award worthy.' However, for those who have had the good fortune of watching *It's a Wonderful Life,* few would disagree that Stewart's performance of George Bailey has been indelibly etched in their hearts and minds, including me.

As great a performance Stewart gave in *It's a Wonderful Life*, the overarching theme of this book and, in part, the motivating force that drove my desire to pen this book does not only originate from his performance. Ironically, the performer who serves as a most fitting paradigm to illustrate the themes captured throughout the pages of this book is Mr. Robert J. Anderson. Anderson was the child actor who played Little George, the young George Bailey. Anderson was born on June 6, 1933 and the release date of *It's a Wonderful Life* was December 20, 1946.

Author's soliloquy:

You may be wondering, who cares about Robert J. Anderson, and who cares whether or not he gave a brilliant performance? The next opportunity that presents itself, look closely, look purposefully at Anderson's performance... really, look very intently at how he conveys his character and brings him to life; the details matter and tell the story. When I was a child watching Anderson's riveting performance, I was immediately teleported into their world—more specifically, teleported into Little George's world. I remember sitting in front of the television even as an adult [approximately 29 years old], thinking "Wow!!! This kid was an amazing actor."

Walk with me as we metaphorically review the tape: Look at how Little George's words, his lines effortlessly dance with the lines of his co-stars, as they exchange the dialogue baton back and forth. Pause and appreciate the seemingly perfect cadence and tempo of their dialogue.

Doesn't Little George look comfortable in his role!?! I believe it's safe to say the execution of his performance looks very comfortable. We also know that a certain level of comfort (being comfortable) in just about any endeavor where our attention is focused breeds confidence. Confidence coupled with intentional practice and repetition breeds grace, command, and ultimately proficiency. Little George also has a certain intangible precocity about himself. Don't fail to notice the conspicuous command he has of each of his lines—observe the sharp clarity that permeates his scene discourse, each and every word. Pay close attention to the gracefulness in which his dialogue glides without a hitch.

From the perspective of development, it is a process each of us can identify with from our own experiences— think of your own development as a child. One can also logically conclude Robert J. Anderson had taken the time to hone his craft over time through diligent study and through his practical experiences. The environment in which he was raised (i.e., his parents' and extended family's tutelage, his teachers/instructors, his education, available resources, his peers' influence, etc.), prior to his role in *It's a Wonderful Life*, naturally molded him into a noticeably precocious person by the time it was time for the camera to roll. A June 8, 2008 *Los Angeles Times* article titled *Child actor played early George Bailey* helped put Anderson's early beginnings in proper context:

> Anderson was born… to a Hollywood family. His father, Gene Anderson, was involved in production at Columbia Pictures, and his uncle, William Beaudine,

was a prolific director. Bobbie Anderson first appeared on screen as a toddler and went on to roles in the 1940s Shirley Temple movie "Young People," "A Tree Grows in Brooklyn" (1945) and "The Bishop's Wife" (1947), among others. He also appeared on TV, including a supporting role to Disney's "Spin and Marty" characters in the 1950s.

The fact that Anderson had family members who worked in the movie industry, I suspect, didn't hurt his development; it only added to it. In addition, his acting opportunities leading up to his portrayal of Little George in *It's a Wonderful Life* served as invaluable boot camps.

Losing ourselves to experience a world outside of our own through the movie screen; isn't that the purpose of movies? Mr. Anderson's portrayal of Little George was nothing short of spectacular in my mind. Mr. Anderson, like many actors, lost himself to play the unforgettable role of Little George. As I watched Little George in *It's a Wonderful Life,* his performance was so wonderfully done that I lost myself, left my world, and met Little George in his world to walk with him on his journey within the movie—indeed, Anderson's unique *Genius* shined very brightly during his performance.

Based on miles and miles of extensive research we have read, seen on television and multitudes of insightful non-fiction material we have readily available to us all, is there a way to replicate the same formula for brilliance and *Genius,* mirror the same formula for facility in expression, and reproduce the same formula for nimble, agile skill we clearly see in Anderson, as he portrayed Little George, in *every* child and adult alike? As great a performance Anderson gave when he portrayed Little George, his performance should not surprise us. We've seen prodigies and savants on the television show *60 Minutes* or similar broadcasts. Study after study has shown how incredible and dynamic the minds of children are and can be—studies have shown how extraordinary the human mind is, full stop.

If you need another example of a young adult performing giftedly, look no further than Ms. Natalie Portman's portrayal of a 12-year old girl and apprentice named Mathilda Lando in the French film *Léon: The Professional*. The film was released in France on September 14, 1994 and in the United States on November 18, 1994. Similar to Robert J. Anderson, Portman's portrayal of Mathilda was also filled with glaring precocity. As a movie enthusiast, I believe the elements that also made Portman's portrayal such an extraordinary one, in addition to her precociousness, were her uncanny charm, and arguably, her unmatched acting and emotional range during her performance at such a young age. Very simply said, she had the "acting chops" of a—quite extraordinary—seasoned veteran *adult* actor when she was only in preadolescence. If we analyze Ms. Portman in a vacuum, her precocity may seem atypical.

When learning more about Ms. Portman's rearing, relationship with her parents and overall life journey, it helped me to better understand and develop an even deeper appreciation of the unique Genius conveyed through her talent as an actor. The following snippets from *Natalie Portman – an unofficial biography* written by Jutze provide more insight in that regard:

Natalie Ward was born on Tuesday, June 9th 1981 in Jerusalem, actually on her mother's birthday. […] She was the first and only child of her parents. Her Israeli father is an infertility specialist and works as a doctor. Her American mother is a full-time homemaker.

When she was three, her family moved to the US, because her father did his residency in Maryland. At the age of four[,] she started taking dancing lessons and she remembers "I've always loved entertaining people and putting on shows at home." (TV Hits Magazine 2/1997). She also took some singing lessons and she recalls: "I was definitely heading more down the Broadway route. I wanted to be in "Oklahoma!" or something. I wasn't thinking of films at all." (Star Wars Insider #44 5/1999).

Her father started his fellowship three years later in Connecticut, so they had to move again. It made her "more able to adjust to new people and make new friends easily. […] ….since her dad is Israeli[,] she grew up with a different set of values than most American kids. This would become obvious in her self-confident decisions and her future career as [an] actress. Looking back she remarks[,] "I don't even remember who my friends were before I was nine." It was then that her father became a doctor and started working in New York. […] The only stable constitution was her family.

This explains why there has always been a strong bond between her and her parents. Concerning this constellation, Natalie says "[y]ou really learn to function as an adult." Even before her movie career took off[,] forcing her family to seek refuge in their privacy, they spen[t] a lot of time together. "I am an only child. All [of] my vacations are with my parents." (Vanity Fair #465 5/1999) She visited countries like Japan and Australia with them in her childhood days, [which] definitely had an impact on her. Later she'd take Japanese as a subject in school.

I find the launch of Natalie's story, her journey, so to speak, very fascinating. She was born in a tightknit, supportive Jewish family. Due to her father's career in the medical field, her and her family were continuously transient throughout her childhood. Being the only child likely had its advantages and disadvantages. An immediate advantage would be that she would be the only target of her mom and dad's undivided, customized love, wisdom, and guidance. Her interviews are riddled with reflections that acknowledge the depth to which the "strong bond between her and her parents" and the conspicuous amount of time together with them, whether "in the refuge of their privacy [at home]" or during family excursions abroad, taught her how to "function as an adult." She may have not had the typical childhood of most children where she was surrounded by other kids her age the majority of the time during leisure and recreation, which some may argue was a disadvantage. After all, we only have one opportunity in life to truly experience the carefree nature and spirit inherent with childhood. That said, the precocity that can be clearly observed in the French film *Léon: The Professional* is the direct result of the atypical childhood described in her interviews, not in spite of (i.e., an advantage):

> When I was 10 [note: in some interviews she says she was 11] years old, after dance class I went to a pizza parlor and a guy from Revlon was there and he wanted me to model for Revlon. So he introduced me to modeling agents, and I told them "I don't want to model, I want to act," so they introduced me to acting agents." (The Late Show with David Letterman 11/1994) Three summers she spent at theatre camps gaining her first acting experiences playing such roles as Dream Laurey in "Oklahoma!" and Hermia in "A Midsummer Night's Dream."
>
> Eventually she participated at auditions for the role in "The Professional[,]" which she would finally get. At first[,] she was rejected [as] being too young, but after… some more auditions[,] director Luc Besson chose her to play Mathilda Lando [in *Léon: The Professional*].

Mariam Webster defines *boot camp* in the following way: "a program or situation that helps people become much better at doing something in a short period of time." The acting opportunities afforded to Natalie Portman leading up to her role in *Léon: The Professional* were likewise exceedingly advantageous, just as the acting opportunities afforded to Robert J. Anderson leading up to his role in *It's a Wonderful Life* were exceedingly advantageous to him. The three summers she spent at "theatre camps gaining her first acting experiences" were 'boot camps' that helped Natalie become much-much better in a short period of time:

> They [Natalie's parents] talk[ed] to the director for hours before every project I do, to make sure I'm not going to be doing anything that's going to be hurting me in my personal life[.]" (Vanity Fair #465 5/1999) This meant that one of them would accompany her whenever she was filming outside New York, at least until she turned 18. So her mother flew with her to Paris. Her father visited them every other weekend.

> Eventually she adapted Portman (her grandmother's maiden name) as her stage name to protect her family life in case her performance would be unsatisfactory. Obviously[,] this wasn't the case. Still[,] she kept it to protect her privacy as her acting career continued. [...] Shooting [*The Professional*] in New York began on June 1st.... [...] Although she never took [formal] acting lessons[,] her performance is convincing. Her character grows more mature as the plot unwinds and becomes strong and self-confident in the end. Commenting [on] her performance in "The Professional[,]" director Luc Besson states "Natalie had no experience before. The first time we... [saw] one- or two-thousand girls[,] and she was the best. You explain, she listen[s,] and she do[es] it, so simple." (from a commentary video clip around 1994) Natalie story

> Due to her performance in "The Professional[,"] Natalie didn't have to go to auditions along with her other candidates any longer. Instead[,] producers approached her with roles and scripts.

In the movie industry, when an actor reaches a stratosphere where he or she no longer has to audition and instead is approached by producers with roles and scripts, that means that actor has established a name for themselves. That is exactly what Portman did, based on her extraordinary performance in *The Professional*. Natalie Portman's journey encompassed, amongst other elements, an ideal mix of unique *Genius*, focused *passion*, personal drive, training, self-development, wise counseling, and opportunities. Her parents' thoughtful guidance and hands on management were instrumental during the early phases of her career. When I read the preceding interview, I found the director's impression of Portman very insightful. Director, Luc Besson, appears to have been equally in awe of her acting talent, her unique acting *Genius,* and unique acting *fingerprint*, so to speak, as I was when I first saw her performance. By my fuzzy recollection, I was in high school when I first saw *The Professional,* and I was completely enchanted by every aspect of Portman's performance. As I watched, I was absolutely riveted the entire time. Fast forward several movies and years later, "[i]n 2011, [Portman] won both the Golden Globe Award and the Academy Award for Best Actress" in the Darren Aronofsky's 2010 film, *Black Swan.*

The beauty and poetry in *Everyone is an Einstein; and There is an Einstein in Everyone* is that this book, this tool—perspective is key—I envision, will serve as a source of inspiration, encouragement, and change for the good. Children, more specifically, *every* child is a gift to our world and should be given an opportunity to (1) discover their respective unique *Genius*, (2) develop their unique

Genius, (3) maximize their potential through the lens of their unique *Genius,* and also (4) contribute their unique *fingerprints* (i.e., unique imagination, unique creativity, unique talent, unique physical ability, etc.) to affect the ever-changing challenges that we face in the twenty-first century and beyond, or offer it freely in any manner they choose. That means your child, my child, *every* child; the same rings true for *every* adult *(i.e., everyone)*. When the phrase 'every child and adult alike' is used throughout the pages of this book, that phrase is not limited to only children and adults living in the United States. The ideas expressed throughout these pages are universal and inclusive of every child and every adult on every continent on this planet. The thoughts contained in every Amendment of this book are my efforts to leave an impactful legacy. Genesis 4:9 in the New International Version *Bible* states: "Then the Lord said to Cain, 'Where is your brother Abel?' 'I don't know,' he replied. 'Am I my brother's keeper?'" I can't speak for Cain; neither can I speak for you. However, my personal answer to that question is an emphatic, **Yes I Am!** In the words of Peter Benenson:

> **It is "[b]etter to light a candle than curse the darkness."**

This book is my light to the proverbial candle, my offering to our world. I encourage you to also add your light to the candle!

AMENDMENT II

Infinite Human Potential (Part 2)

"NOT EVERYTHING THAT CAN BE COUNTED
COUNTS AND NOT EVERYTHING THAT COUNTS
CAN BE COUNTED."

—ALBERT EINSTEIN

Speaking from the perspective of a world society, a person's ability to maximize his or her infinite potential inevitably affects each of us and affects all of us collectively at some point in time. Why is that important? We live in an interdependent world. The National Geography Standard, *Geography Standard 11: The Patterns and Networks of Economic Interdependence on Earth's Surface* explains:

> Resources are evenly distributed on Earth, and no country has all of the resources it needs to survive and grow independently. Thus, people must trade with others in increasingly complex global economic networks.

> Economic activities depend upon capital, resources, energy, labor, information, and land. The spatial

patterns of resources create the networks of trade and economic interdependence that exist at local, regional, national, and international scales. Local and world economies mesh to create networks, movement patterns, transportation routes, communications systems, markets, and hinterlands.

Subsistence farming often exists side by side with commercial agriculture. In many developing countries, millions of people leave rural areas for cities in search of jobs, some of which have been outsourced from industrialized countries. Technology and telecommunications have freed many jobs from being tied to specific locations. Work can be done collaboratively in different locations, taking advantage of different time zones to increase efficiency.

As world population grows, as energy costs increase, as time becomes more valuable, as resources become depleted or discovered, and as new products meet new demands, economic systems need to be more efficient and responsive.

The economic success, or not, of people of different nations, who live on opposite sides of the equator and across the globe is important to me; being informed and not woefully ignorant of the reality of our interdependence is not an option. There is good reason why our collective global economic success should also be important to you. The National Geography Standards Index, "*Geography is for Life in Every Sense of that Expression: Lifelong, Life-Sustaining, and Life Enhancing*" sets the stage:

Understanding and responding to the challenges and opportunities of the world in the twenty-first century will require many skills; the capacities to think and communicate mathematically and scientifically will remain at a premium. [...] As individuals and as members of society, humans face decisions on where to live, what to build where, how and where to travel, how to conserve energy, how to wisely manage scarce resources, and how to cooperate or compete with others.

Making all of these decisions, personal and collective, requires a geographically informed person—someone who sees meaning in the arrangement of things on Earth's surface, who sees relations between people, places, and environments, who uses geographic skills, and who applies spatial and ecological perspectives to life situations.

It is very clear how the concept of interdependence affects our global community from an economic perspective. It's not only significant for the people in my particular country of citizenship (i.e., the United States) to maximize their infinite potential, the same also rings true for people in countries outside my own. The entire planet benefits from the sum total of innovation, creativity, and Genius that are the fruits of our passions, intrigue, and labor. My intention within the pages of this book is not necessarily to write a thesis on the future of the global economy. However, I believe it is vastly important to connect the dots (CTD) that directly capture the existing need for a more conscious (self and combined conscious), more strategic, more aspirational pursuit to maximize the infinite human potential of not only the children and adults immediate to you and I, but also the children and adults across the globe. Remarks at the Brookings Institute's *US-Japan Forum: Challenges for the Global Economy and a Better Globalization* spotlighted the arduous, but collectively manageable test before us:

In recent years, a remarkable backlash against globalization has been observed in many parts of the world. Britain voted to leave the EU [European Union]. The U.S. administration has an 'America First' slogan. Recent elections in France, Germany, and Italy show the rise of public support for anti-globalization policies. At the same time, international cooperation to address global challenges has seen major milestones through the Addis Ababa Action Agenda, UN Sustainable Development Goals, and the Paris Agreement on Climate Change. Moving towards a better globalization must address three challenges. It must promote a revival of global growth with broad-based social advancement. It must foster innovation and the development of technology [,] while tackling any adverse effects on work and combating rising inequality. It must deliver on the energy and climate agenda before the window for limiting global warming to less than 2 degrees closes.

Many countries are experiencing worsening inequality, inadequate job creation and increased unemployment among the youth. The concerns about inequality are coupled with how to create more employment and how to protect those adversely affected by technological change. National policies will matter, but there is also the question about the role of the multilateral community in supporting much better technological diffusion and helping countries create the conditions to tap the opportunities from technological change.

Many solutions require global cooperation. There is a need to mobilize various players both domestic and global in an inclusive manner, and not only economically, but also politically and socially as well. No government alone can deliver the climate goals and at the same time, no single president can stop the progress.

The future of our global economy depends on *You*. There is unique *Genius* within each of us that can be used to benefit our world over. While I am not an economist, a master's degree in economics is not required to understand the correlation between the aspirational goal of maximizing infinite human potential and global interdependence. Regardless of whether you live in North America, South America, Africa, Europe, Asia, or Australia, as human beings, our lives are inextricably linked and are equally significant. As imperative as it is for each of us to understand the concept of interdependence from an economic perspective, I believe it is more imperative for each of us to understand the concept of interdependence from a basic human perspective, as we humanely, empathetically, and compassionately see ourselves and our respective hopes and dreams in the eyes of others, as others humanely, empathetically, and compassionately see themselves and their respective hopes and dreams in the eyes of each of us.

The book *The Art of Happiness in a Troubled World*, chapter two, titled "Me and We," further adds to the discussion of interdependence very astutely. *The Art of Happiness in a Troubled World* is authored by His Holiness The Dalai Lama and Howard C. Cutler, M.D. On the inside flap of the front dust jacket, it states that "Dr. Howard Cutler walks readers through the Dalai Lama's philosophy on how to achieve peace of mind.... Together, the two examine the roots of many of the problems facing the world and show us how we can approach these calamities...." Much of the book is written in dialogue form between The Dalai Lama and Dr. Cutler:

> "Your Holiness, yesterday we were speaking about this problem of people feeling isolated and the benefits of this sense of community, I began, "so, essentially, what we are talking about here is identifying with a wider group, kind of moving from the focus on 'me' to the focus on 'we'".... you've often mentioned how you feel that our connection to others, relating to others with human affection, a sense of caring and compassion and so on, is integral to personal happiness...."
>
> "Well," I continued, "I think there could be a potential problem. Certainly it is natural that people may strongly identify with their particular group or community. But this can highlight our differences from other groups, which can often lead to a feeling of superiority. Strong group identification not only produces pride for one's own group[,] but also creates the very real potential of developing bias and prejudice against other groups. So, the question is, how can one encourage the transition from 'I' to 'Us,' moving from a feeling of isolation to a feeling of identification with a group, yet prevent that

from progressing to 'Us' against 'Them'? It seems that human beings have a long history of that kind of thing occurring, and from there[,] it is a very short step to conflict and even violence."

"This is true," the Dalai Lama agreed; "that is why it is important to recognize... that there can be different levels to the concept of 'community'—and I think it is important that one's cultural or national identity, or whatever, does not override one's basic identity as a human being, as also being a member of the human community. This is critical."

".... we are talking about connecting on a deeper level, on the basic human level, connecting with others based on that fundamental human bond[—t]he absence of that fundamental human bond can result in a sense of indifference, a lack of concern for others' welfare that can in turn lead to problems...."

The question is whether we relate to others based on what differentiates us or on the characteristics we share. This can determine whether we have an underlying sense of separation from others, or a feeling of affinity and a bond to a wider community.

To have a real sense of brotherhood, sisterhood, based on identifying oneself first and foremost as a human being is not easy. It doesn't happen overnight. But I feel that part of the problem is that in day-to-day life, the majority of people don't give serious thought to their common connection to all other human beings. They do not spend time reflecting on it. ….in society there is much greater emphasis on our individual differences. …. their connection to others is normally not so apparent. Yet[,] that human bond is always there.

From the perspective of the global *human bond*, the global *brotherhood/sisterhood,* and the global *community (family)*, that is the standpoint from which *Everyone is an Einstein*; and *There is an Einstein in Everyone* is written. The hopes and unlimited future *I* desire for *me* are the same hopes and unlimited future *I* desire for *you*; and as the term The Dalai Lama so eloquently used, the same hopes *I* desire for "*Us*". The only substantive *thing* that truly separates me, you, and those the world over (i.e., "*Us*") is the physical proximity in the world *we* live in.

* * * *

The human mind and how its circuitry operates; the process, change, and development that takes place, that transforms the mind of a nascent to that of a mature thinker and doer (e.g., Natalie Portman); the mechanics that occur that generate the mildest of thought and transform it into the brightest, most creative of ideas; and how the integrated network of the brain establishes initial thought pathways and dredges new, more nuanced, more intricate intellect highways have intrigued me since my college years. More specifically, my intrigue noticeably began during my Psychology 101 course. I was naturally enamored when learning about the concept of neuroplasticity years later.

Neuroplasticity is a fascinating area of research—one of several linchpins that reinforce the overarching motif of this book (i.e., *Everyone is an Einstein*; and *There is an Einstein in Everyone)*. The research on neuroplasticity touches on the endless potential of the human mind due to its ability to adapt to its environment and re-adapt to new environments, new experiences, and new stimuli. An immediate example of neuroplasticity in action (as discussed earlier) is illustrated through a combination of how Portman's early acting opportunities (i.e., training/*boot camp*) and noticeably close relationship with her parents sculpted her unique *Genius,* talent, and ability in the realm of acting. She spent, in a social context, an uncommonly enormous amount of time with her parents in contrast to the typical parent child relationship. Her unique *Genius,* talent, and ability adapted to her environment, and as a result, she delivered us the brilliant performance available for everyone to view in the French film *Léon: The Professional.*

In her book, *Train Your Mind Change Your Brain*, author Sharon Begley provides an exceedingly thoughtful and insightful analysis of the deficiencies in pre-neuroplasticity thinking and the reason for optimism, based on documented research and experiments associated with neuroplasticity. "[T]he received dogma in neuroscience for a century had held that the brain takes its shape for life during our childhood years and does not change its structure thereafter," noted Daniel Goleman in the preface he wrote for Ms. Begley's book. As a teenager, I remember reading several books and watching numerous news stories on television that reaffirmed this antiquated frame of thought or "*dogma*"—at the time, I unfortunately believed that "*dogma*," considering I don't remember reading research that outlined refutations.

According to Goleman, ".... that assumption has joined countless others in the trash heap of scientific 'givens' that the march of research has forced us to discard. Neuroscience now has a vibrant branch exploring the many ways the brain continues to reshape itself throughout life." Further on in her book, Ms. Begley noted the following:

> The textbook wisdom held that the adult brain is hard-wired, fixed in form and function, so that by the time you reach adulthood, we are pretty much stuck with what we have.

> But the dogma is wrong. In the last years of the twentieth century, a few iconoclastic neuroscientists challenged the paradigm that the adult brain cannot change and made discovery after discovery that, to the contrary, it retains stunning powers of neuroplasticity. The brain can indeed be rewired.

> .... [T]he brain can change its physical structure and its wiring long into adulthood.

> In response to actions and experiences of its owner, a brain forges stronger connections in circuits that under-lie one behavior or thought and weakens the connec-tions in others. Most of this happens because of what we do and what we experience of the outside world. In this sense, the very structure of our brain—the relative size of different regions, the strength of connections

between one area and another—reflects the lives we have led.

The excerpt that I cited in the preamble of this book with respect to the Eagle and chicken is captured in John C. Maxwell's book, *Talent is Never Enough*. It touches on the importance of believing in our respective potential. Maxwell also uses the following additional quotes to undergird his main premise, which are also applicable here. The first quote is from Ms. Sharon Wood:

> We often put too much emphasis on mere physical challenges and obstacles, and give too little credence to psychological and emotional ones. Sharon Wood, the first North American women to climb Mount Everest, learned some things about that after making her successful climb. She said, "I discovered it wasn't a matter of physical strength, but a matter of psychological strength. The conquest laid within my own mind to penetrate those barriers of self-imposed limitations and get through to that good stuff—the stuff called potential, 90 percent of which we rarely use."

The second quote uses the following comparison offered by cartoonist, Charles Schulz:

> "Life is a ten-speed bike. Most of us have gears we never use."

There are times when we can be our own worst enemies, simply by how much or how little we think about and value ourselves. However, we can also be our own best friends, simply by how much positive intrinsic value we consciously allow to reverberate within and how favorably we think of ourselves. The science of neuroplasticity provides evidence that we can unlearn unhealthy thinking habits and that our minds have limitless capacities to overlearn healthy thinking habits. The human mind is simply an extraordinary machine. Through the science of neuroplasticity, we understand that we can train our minds to do virtually anything—in the words Maxwell uses to quote Thomas Edison in *Talent is Never Enough*, "If we did all the things we are capable of doing, we would literally astonish ourselves."

Based on the study of neuroplasticity, it's not mere speculation or lofty rhetoric to state that the potential of every human being is infinite. In the words of Zig Ziglar, "[w]here you start is not as important as where you finish." Regardless of where we begin our respective journeys, where we find ourselves on our respective journeys today, and how many times we may choose to reinvent ourselves during the course of our respective journeys, the unique *Genius* within each of us is perpetually being sculpted by what we *do* and what we *experience* of the outside world. I've heard it said that "[t]he journey is more important than the destination." Having a firm understanding of this concept, when reading the story of Christopher Langan, "who many call the smartest man in America," I was riveted in every sense of the word by the life changing *experiences* that had occurred throughout his life and what he had done to respond to those *experiences*, which significantly shaped, steered the trajectory his journey ultimately would take. Langan's story, as told by Malcom Gladwell, fittingly embodies the morphing, the manifestations of neuroplasticity.

Malcom Gladwell is one of the extraordinary *Geniuses*, thinkers, writers, authors of our time. In his book *Outliers: The Story of Success*, in part, Mr. Gladwell surgically dissected the genesis of several of the world's most remarkably accomplished entrepreneurs (e.g., Bill Gates) and artists (e.g., The Beatles), which broadened our "understanding of [the mechanics and underpinnings that lead to] success...." Every chapter in *Outliers* is replete with thought-provoking analyses, coupled with countless tables brimming with food for thought—the chapters that were the most spellbinding and riveting to me were chapters Three and Four. The title of chapter Three is: "The Trouble with Geniuses, Part 1, Knowledge of a Boy's IQ is of Little Help if You are Faced with a Formful of Clever Boys". The title of chapter Four is: "The Trouble with Geniuses, Part 2, After Protracted Negotiations, It Was Agreed that Robert Would be Put on Probation". In part, chapters Three and Four spotlight the story and significance of Mr. Chris Langan in relation to Mr. Gladwell's overarching endeavor to demystify what takes place before achieving extraordinary levels of success to the degree that one (or a group) becomes "a true outlier(s)...."

As Mr. Gladwell so eloquently conveyed, ironically, being extraordinarily intelligent and the man ".... who many call the smartest man in America" aren't necessarily reliable indicators of who eventually succeeds nor who ultimately achieves astonishing levels of success—there's far more to it, and Mr. Langan's story is the epitome of this idea. The purpose of the paragraphs that follow is not to retell the story of Chris Langan nor further compare and contrast the experiences of Chris Langan versus Robert Oppenheimer beyond the superlative job done by Mr. Gladwell. However, additional bite-size observations are provided as food for thought.

For readers who aren't as familiar with Mr. Langan's story, Mr. Gladwell begins chapter Three of his book *Outliers* by introducing us to Mr. Lagan, as he appeared as a special guest on the quiz show *1 vs. 100*:

> In the fifth episode of the 2008 season[, a]t stake is a million dollars. The guest has to be smart enough to answer more questions correctly than his or her one hundred adversaries—and by that standard, few have ever seemed as superbly qualified as Christopher Langan.

In an attempt to briefly capture some of the remaining details Mr. Gladwell uses to describe Mr. Langan's experience on *1 vs. 100*, consider the following:

> Out strode Langan onto the stage amid wild applause.

> "You don't think you need to have a high intellect to do well on *One versus One Hundred*, do you?" the show's host, Bob Saget, asked him. Saget looked at Langan oddly, as if he were some kind of laboratory specimen.

As Mr. Gladwell moves on in his story, he explains:

> Over the past decade, Chris Langan has achieved a strange kind of fame. He has become the public face

of genius in American life, a celebrity outlier. He gets invited on news shows and profiled in magazines, and he has been the subject of a documentary by the filmmaker Errol Morris, all because of a brain that appears to defy description.

Gladwell continues:

On the set of *1 vs. 100*, Langan was poised and confident. His voice was deep. His eyes were small and fiercely bright. He did not circle about topics, searching for the right phrase, or double back to restate a previous sentence. For that matter, he did not say um, or ah, or use any form of conversational mitigation: his sentences came marching out, one after another, polished and crisp, like soldiers on a parade ground. Every question Saget threw at him, he tossed aside, as if it were a triviality. When his winnings reached $250,000, he appeared to make a mental calculation that the risks of losing everything were at that point greater than the potential benefits of staying in. Abruptly, he stopped. "I'll take the cash," he said. He shook Saget's hand firmly and was finished—exiting on top as, we like to think, geniuses invariably do.

I'm not sure how you feel or felt immediately after reading Mr. Gladwell's preceding narrative regarding Langan's *1 vs. 100* appearance. I was buttoned to my chair and found his scene by scene narrative captivating in every sense. I also watched the entire clip of Mr. Langan's *1 vs. 100* appearance on YouTube—if you have not had the opportunity to view it, I highly recommend it. As I watched very closely, very intently, I thought, with an IQ as off the charts as his, what kind of inductive and deductive reasoning did he process first, and what if, then statements did he internally toil through before answering the questions?

During the research collection phase of authoring this book, I learned that many aspects of Mr. Langan's life were and are very similar to the "average person." During the course of his adult life, "the smartest man in America" served in a variety of labor-intensive jobs, such as a construction worker, cowboy, forest service firefighter, and farmhand; he also served as a bouncer in Long Island, New York for over 20 years. By the time Mr. Gladwell arrives at the conclusion of his anecdote with respect to Mr. Langan, we learn that Mr. Langan [in his fifties] and his wife had settled into a modest life ".... in rural Missouri on a horse farm." Furthermore, "Lagan seemed content. He had farm animals to take care of, and books to read, and a wife he loved. It was a much better life than being a bouncer."

Let the record reflect that in no way am I saying there is anything wrong, in any sense, with Mr. Langan ultimately choosing to live a ".... modest life in Missouri on a horse farm." For many people, a modest life is optimal. That said, based on Mr. Gladwell's account, we learn that Mr. Langan had wanted more for himself than, *by himself*, he was able to achieve. Mr. Langan's ".... principal occupation [was a bouncer] for much of his adult years." Gladwell continues:

Through it all, he continued to read deeply in philosophy, mathematics, and physics as he worked on a sprawling treatise he calls the "CTMU"—the

"Cognitive Theoretic Model of the Universe [CTMU]."
But without academic credentials, he despairs of ever
getting published in a scholarly journal.

As I read this section of *Outliers*, admittedly, I was saddened
by Mr. Langan's story; although he was (is) obviously gifted
and patently intelligent in every sense of the words "gifted"
and "intelligent," his conspicuous talents, intelligence, and
Genius, regardless of how brilliant he had taught himself
to be, were literally not enough to accomplish some of his
ambitious goals. Mr. Gladwell continues:

> It is a heartbreaking story. At one point I asked Lan-
> gan—hypothetically—whether he would take a job at
> Harvard University were it offered to him. "Well, that's
> a difficult question," he replied. "Obviously, as a full
> professor at Harvard[,] I would count. My ideas would
> have weight and I could use my position, my affiliation
> at Harvard, to promote my ideas. An institution like
> that is a great source of intellectual energy, and if I
> were at a place like that, I could absorb the vibration
> in the air." It was suddenly clear how lonely his life has
> been. Here he was, a man with an insatiable appetite
> for learning, forced for most of his adult life to live in
> intellectual isolation. "I even noticed that kind of intel-
> lectual energy in the year and a half I was in college," he
> said, almost wistfully. "Ideas are in the air constantly.
> It's such a stimulating place to be.["]

Prior to reading *Outliers*, I, personally, was not familiar
with the unique *Genius* and story of Christopher Langan.
It's highly likely that similar to me, when hearing only a

fraction of Mr. Langan's story for the very first time, you may have had invariably the same reaction and many of the same questions that I did. Considering the enormous expanse of intellectual gold Mr. Langan refined over the years through his own self-study, self-persistence, and self-development, one would think: why isn't he leading the group of scientists working assiduously in research to find a cure for AIDS, cancer or any of the other catastrophic, insidious diseases that affect our world over; why hasn't he been summoned to contribute to some of the major fields of physics research (i.e., condensed matter physics; atomic, molecular, and optical physics; particle physics; astrophysics; geophysics or biophysics, etc.); or why hasn't he been recruited to assist with the altruistic, yet arduous endeavor of revamping the current public school curriculum, testing standards, and learning paradigms here in the United States and in support of other countries around the world? If you are a United States congressman/congresswoman, University Professor, and/or someone leading a private or public organization reading this, it is not too late to reach out to Mr. Langan, just in case he is interested.

Educational institutions—from prekindergarten to postgraduate and beyond—the world over could and would benefit immensely from Mr. Christopher Langan's insights with respect to better understanding how we learn and devising techniques and strategies to more effectively teach from an instructor perspective and, with more efficacy, to self-teach from a personal self-development perspective. Bear in mind, this is the man who, at age 3, had "taught himself to read." Mr. Gladwell discussed Mr. Langan's intellectual prowess in great detail throughout the pages of chapter three in *Outliers*:

> [Mr. Langan] was speaking at six months of age.

> "The average person has an IQ of one hundred," …. "[Albert] Einstein one fifty. Chris has an IQ of one ninety-five."

Mr. Langan's "score was literally off the charts—too high to be accurately measured" when an IQ test was conducted by "[t]he television news show 20/20." He also "…. took an IQ test specially designed for people too smart for ordinary IQ tests" for which "[h]e got all the questions right except one." If you need more proof of his vastly remarkable intelligence, consider the following. On the Scholastic Assessment Test (SAT), he achieved a perfect score, "even though he fell asleep at one point during the test." According to Mr. Langan's brother Mark, with respect to Langan's summer routine in high school, "[h]e did math for an hour[.] […] Then he did French for an hour. Then he studied Russian. Then he would read philosophy. He did that religiously, every day.

Mr. Langan's aptitude and intellect are quite extraordinary—from a personal self-development perspective, why wouldn't each of us desire to glean from someone with his gritty background, of his impressive fortitude, and of his intellectual heft. Regardless of where you may reside on this planet, the fact is that everyone will not have the good fortune of acquiring the benefits of a wise mentor, whom devotes focused, customized time and energy to their development. Everyone does not and will not have the luxury of highly educated parents, whom can provide or, if necessary, attain the most optimal learning tools and resources and create an atmosphere at home that is the most encouraging, inspiring and conducive for learning. We understand that teachers (i.e., inclusive of prekindergarten instructors through university level professors) are human and, their respective abilities to effectively teach, mold, and enrich the minds of their pupils vary largely based on their corresponding levels of competency and dexterity in the art of communication coupled with their passion to wade through the rigors of effectively inculcating the subject area they teach. In addition, the fact is that although the Government and school superintendents continually work tirelessly to improve low performing schools and refurbish dilapidated educational institutions at the national, state and local levels, until that is a reality for everyone, the quality of schools differs depending on the zip code or place on Earth you live.

My focus throughout this book will be on each human being's ability to self-develop (i.e., self-train) via the processes of self-awareness, self-direction/self-management, self-confidence coupled with humility, self-exploration, self-discovery, self-expansion, and continuous self-analysis. My goal in writing this book is not to identify or propose a panacea of some sort; in part, my strategy is to spotlight how much ability, focus, *Genius each of us have* within to shape our respective destinies. Our willingness to see ourselves in the eyes and hearts of each other, and then choose to assist each other from that perspective during our

respective journeys with a greater sense of social consciousness and social awareness will also contribute to the extent
to which each of us achieve our *'full potentials.'*

Mr. Gladwell uses the early upbringing and an intrigu-
ingly pivotal period in Mr. Robert Oppenheimer's life to
illustrate how his story is the antithesis of Mr. Langan's.
Unlike Mr. Oppenheimer, the average person won't have
an opportunity to attend the Ethical Cultural Fieldstone
School in New York City, where "students were [and are]
'infused with the notion that they were being groomed to
reform the world.'" As a society, we understand that certain
privileges are only available to the privileged. *Concerted
cultivation* "is a style of parenting that is marked by a parent's attempts to foster their child's talent by incorporating
organized activities in their children's lives"—it would be
a privilege if every child could nurture and cultivate their
intellectual development and intellectual capacities, under
the umbrella of a concerted cultivation parenting style.
However, that is not an option for many underprivileged
children. Everyone doesn't possess a *"cultural* advantage" in
the sense of coming from an educated middle to upper class
family who "....painstakingly taught them [...] through
the technique of concerted cultivation...[by] nudging and
prodding and encouraging and showing [them] the rules
of the game...." of life. Everyone isn't trained from childhood to have an overabundance of the combination of
analytical intelligence, practical intelligence, learned social
savvy, charm, social agility and nimbleness as Mr. Robert
Oppenheimer—this is not meant from a social introvert/
social extrovert perspective.

Mr. Gladwell astutely noted that "…. no one—not rock stars, not professional athletes, not software billionaires, and not even geniuses—ever makes it alone." According to Mr. Gladwell, with respect to successfully navigating through the jagged, bumpy terrain of intellectual development, personal achievement, and life in general, Mr. Langan "…. had to make it alone." However, many friends of yours and many friends of mine, people who may have been abused (or are being abused), children who may have been raised in poor communities (or are being raised in poor communities), who attend under-resourced schools, children in general, and adults alike are relegated to endeavoring to "making it alone." In the real world where many are placed in a position to "make it alone," what practical lessons can we glean, can we walk away with, can we stitch into the fabric of our collective moral and social consciousness, and zigzag into the social psyche of our collective human culture from Mr. Langan's story?

I read a book that contained an interesting quote from a teacher, and I wonder to what degree it applies to Mr. Langan's journey. Keep in mind that teachers/professors have the ultimate trusted responsibility and good-faith duty to facilitate the education of our children and adults alike. In the book, *The Brain that Changes Itself: Stories of Personal Triumph from the Frontiers of Brain Science*, author Norman Doidge, M.D. references an unfortunate exchange between Michael Merzenich's mother and her first cousin. Mr. Merzenich is a professor emeritus neuroscientist credited with an enormously wide body of work in brain plasticity. Here is Mr. Doidge's account:

When Merzenich was a boy, his mother's first cousin, a grade-school teacher in Wisconsin, was chosen teacher of the year for the entire United States. After the ceremony at the White House, she visited the Merzenich family in Oregon.

"My mother," he recalls, "asked the inane question that you'd ask in conversation: 'What are your most important principles in teaching?' And her cousin answered, 'Well, you test them when they come into school, and you figure out if they are worthwhile. And if they are worthwhile, you really pay attention to them, and you don't waste time on the ones that aren't.' That's what she [teacher of the year for the entire United States at the time] said. [...] ....in one way or another, that's reflected in how people have treated people who are different, forever. It's so destructive to imagine that your neurological resources are permanent and enduring and cannot be substantially improved and altered."

I'm sure when Christopher Langan tested throughout his schooling, he consistently scored off the charts. However, I wonder if his teachers/professors all thought he was "*worthwhile*?" If you're a teacher/professor reading this book, ponder the following:

Do you consider and approach all students in your class as if each is "*worthwhile*," as if each is an *Einstein (Genius)*?

Are students required to test "off the chart" before you personally consider them "*worthwhile*?"

A '*diamond in the rough*' is "[s]omeone (or something) that has hidden exceptional characteristics and/or future potential, but currently lacks the final touches that would make them (or it) truly stand out from the crowd. The phrase is metaphorical and relates to the fact that naturally occurring diamonds are quite ordinary at first glance, and that their true beauty as jewels is only realized through the cutting and polishing process." Aren't we all 'diamonds in the rough,' who, through the vicissitudes and experiences of life, are continuously being cut and polished, re-cut and re-polished... re-cut and re-polished, re-cut and re-polished to be the brightest, most refined diamond that we truly can be? Take the time to consider your own personal story. How deep and in what ways did many of your early adversities and crucibles cut you and shape you, and then re-cut you, re-shaped you, and polished you into the diamond that you are today, though a diamond with an *unfinished finish*? Christopher Langan was a *perfectly imperfect* diamond with an *unfinished finish*, marked by a few blemishes and scuffs of abuse from his childhood, coupled with a few rough edges, considering his maybe underdeveloped social savvy.

How many other Christopher Langan's are out there— that may be unknown, undiscovered, not in an environment nor working in a career that fully maximizes your potential, eager and yearning for an opportunity to share your unique *Genius* with our world, and one or two steps away from an opportunity to change the world with your unique fingerprints? Do you feel intellectually numb during your workday, considering you are not working in a career that you're passionate or curious about, not intrigued with—that concurrently employs your unique Genius to the degree that it engages, excites, and stimulates your "intellectual energy," as Mr. Langan referenced? I suspect many people have either been there at one point or another, even if only very briefly, or are there now.

There is no monetary amount or any 'thing' of value that can adequately quantify or equate to the fulfillment, contentment, and joy that intoxicates a person's mind and spirit when he or she has an opportunity to work, to perform in a capacity for which that person is most *passionate* about, *curious* about, or at a minimum, *intrigued* by. "Not everything that can be counted counts and not everything that counts can be counted" is a quote attributed to Mr. Albert Einstein. When you are doing what you are *passionate* about, *curious* about, *intrigued* by, you are fully engaged, your imagination bulb, creative juices, and mind's eye focus are distinctively heightened, the intellectual energy referenced by Mr. Langan is ignited. In that state, what others may consider work and mundane is perceived by you as stimulating and thrilling, and one hour to someone else performing in that capacity feels like one minute to you, considering how engrossed you are in what you are doing and how resolute you are in manifesting success in what you are endeavoring to accomplish or share. In the same way Mr. Robert J. Anderson lost himself in *It's a Wonderful Life*, one organically loses thyself when working in thy passion. Everyone should have an opportunity to explore their interests and discover what truly intrinsically energizes them—finding our passion(s), what we are curious about or intrigued by can be the beginning of working towards tapping into our infinite potential. Everyone (you) is an Einstein (*Genius*) to the degree we choose to explore, discover, develop, and maximize our respective infinite potential; and the Einstein (*Genius*) in Everyone (you) has the greatest opportunity to thrive and to affect change to the degree our respective unyielding motivations and unwavering inspirations propel us when our unique Genius operates through our *passion*, through our *curiosity*, or by what *intrigues* us.

AMENDMENT III

Albert Einstein
vs.
Christopher Langan

WHO HAD THE "BETTER" MIND?

In our culture, we quite frequently engage in efforts to *compare* people; we seek, generally with innocent intentions, to identify who is considered "the best" or "the greatest" in a particular profession, vocation, sport, (the list goes on and on). As such, oftentimes, the result is the person considered "the best" or "the greatest" is distinguished as somehow *"better"* than the rest of *us*. My personal disposition is that comparing people is toxic and an exercise in futility. Consider the excerpt from John C. Maxwell's book, *Talent is Never Enough,* that begins to illustrate why comparing people is useless:

> Executive coach Joel Garfinkle recounts a story by writer Mark Twain in which a man died and met Saint Peter at the pearly gates. Immediately realizing that Saint Peter was a wise and knowledgeable individual, the man inquired, "Saint Peter, I have been interested

in military history for many years. Tell me[,] who was the greatest general of all time?'

Saint Peter quickly responded, "Oh, that's a simple question. It's that man [or lady] right over there."

"You must be mistaken," responded the man, now very perplexed. "I knew that man on Earth and he was just a common laborer."

"That's right, my friend," assured Saint Peter. "He [or she] would have been the greatest general of all time, if he had been a general."

Although the excerpt references a "man," the overriding thought is inclusive of a premise equally applicable to men and women. How many family members, friends, co-workers, contemporaries do you know who are gifted with innate talents, have been thoroughly trained and, as a result, have developed wide-ranging skill sets, or through their unique life experiences have glaring, undeniable *potential* unique to their person that you are absolutely certain would do exceedingly well performing in careers outside their current choice, *if* only given an opportunity?

Who do you consider the "best" in your particular profession?

The question posited at the beginning of this Amendment inquired, between Mr. Einstein and Mr. Langan, who had the "better" mind?

Take a minute or two to think about your answers. The principal understanding from the preceding Garfinkle excerpt I would like to convey is there truly is no such thing as "better" or "greater," nor is there such thing as "best" when discussing human beings.

Whether working as a CEO, human resource specialist, teacher, chef, professor, television broadcaster, mechanic, or president of a country, the preceding excerpt punctuates that we have only observed the abilities of those who have or have had an opportunity to serve in a variety of roles in our society. There are countless others that walk amongst us who *would*, *could* make us proud with admiration and appreciation at the sight of their Genius in motion in a particular field, *if* given an opportunity to further train, develop, and hone their talents or simply given an opportunity to employ their sharpened, already fully developed (matured) Genius. However, that opportunity never arrives, regardless of whether those reasons are fair or not.

My main thrust through the remainder of this Amendment is to clearly establish why neither Mr. Albert Einstein nor Mr. Christopher Langan is any more of a Genius than you and I and accentuate the folly of comparing human beings. My intent is not to diminish Mr. Einstein's life and accomplishments, nor is it to undervalue Mr. Langan's anomalous intellectual feats. I am, however, conveying the importance of understanding and appreciating the fact that while your Genius, our Genius is *different* from Mr. Einstein's and Mr. Langan's, it is nonetheless priceless in its value and equally endless in its potential.

When the man asked Saint Peter, "…. who was the *greatest* general of all time?", the objective truth is there is no objective truth. The question is unanswerable—there is no objective means to clearly discern "…. who was the *greatest* general of all time" nor who had the *better* mind between Einstein and Langan. Furthermore, although Mr. Einstein is presently thought of as the quintessential *genius*, he is no more and no less of a Genius than Mr. Langan is. Likewise, Mr. Einstein and Mr. Langan are no more and no less of a Genius than you and I are. Mr. Einstein doesn't have a "better" story than Mr. Langan, or vice-versa; Mr. Einstein has a *different* story than Mr. Langan. In the same vein, Mr. Langan doesn't have a "better" mind than Mr. Einstein, or vice-versa; Mr. Langan has a *different* mind than Mr. Einstein—remember, chapter three of the book *Outliers* tells us Mr. Albert Einstein had an IQ of "one fifty," while Mr. Christopher Langan has an IQ of "…one ninety-five… [his score was literally off the charts]…."

One of the many definitions of the word pedestal is "used to describe the position of someone who is admired, successful, etc." People thought of as "geniuses" with a lower case "g" don't generally ask to be placed on pedestals; pop culture and pundits are inclined to take the liberty to place them there. I personally don't place human beings on *pedestals* above me (I believe it's an unhealthy exercise) nor look down upon anyone. That being said, with respect to the definition, I genuinely have *healthy* admiration for the unique details of Mr. Einstein's and Mr. Langan's respective stories equally. I equally value the intellectual depth and range of cognition exhibited by these men. Their personal stories and minds are *no different* from each human being in our solar system in that their personal stories and minds are uniquely *different*; too disparate to compare them to each other or to compare them to us.

Each of us have our own distinctive path we travel during our transit, voyage so to speak, from the beginning of our life, through detours, until the end worthy of its own individual appreciation—as if appreciating art work. We all begin with a brand new, fresh canvas free of wear and tear on which a portrait of our days, nights, and life are eventually stenciled. As each individual life commences, the canvas and pattern gradually become rife with color (various shades of reds, whites, "grays," and also "black-and-blues"), texture, wrinkles, lines (squiggly and straight), complexity, and depth relative to our individual unique circumstances. Some portraits end with no color at all. Our respective paths include culture, relationships, adversity, heartbreaks, triumphs, growth, endurance, and much more. I have reiterated that Albert Einstein and Christopher Langan are no more and no less of a Genius than you and I are. Hearing more of their stories will help you understand the perspective from which I speak.

Albert Einstein had a remarkable life, lavished with numerous awards, major accomplishments, and distinguished honors. When I read biographies, I'm often most fascinated by the details of early childhood. The details of Mr. Einstein's childhood are placed in context in Mr. Walter Isaacson's book, *Einstein*:

> He was slow in learning how to talk. [...] Even after he had begun using words, sometime after the age of 2,

he developed a quirk.... [Einstein had a mild form of echolalia, causing him to repeat phrases to himself....] Whenever he had something to say, he would try it out on himself, whispering it softly until it sounded good enough to pronounce aloud.

His slow development was combined with a cheeky rebelliousness toward authority, which led one schoolmaster to...amuse history by declaring that he would never amount to much.

His cocky contempt for authority led him to question received wisdom in ways that well-trained acolytes... never contemplated. And as for his slow verbal development, he came to believe that it allowed him to observe with wonder the everyday phenomena that others took for granted.

Think about your own personal story. Was there, is there a personal "quirk," style, way to synthesize information, or approach to employ your creativity that lead prior or current instructors, employers or other persons in authority to say you "would never amount to much" or doubt your capability, as with Mr. Einstein? You may have been told your "quirk" was, is a weakness by people who misunderstood, misunderstand your gift (your Genius). In part, the beauty in Mr. Einstein's childhood, and likely yours as well, is the attributes and gifts that rendered him, render you unique, different, special are precisely the necessary tools that equip us to create something new, to offer something unlike anything seen before to our world. Unfortunately, many times, instead of recognizing the immeasurable value in those attributes and gifts, people, while well-meaning at times, tend to misunderstand them (*be aware of that tendency and guard your gift*)—these are the same tools that unearth, sculpt, shape the Genius within. Know yourself; take inventory of what makes you unique; learn about and understand your Genius; and be aware of which environments, which tools amplify and accentuate your Genius and which do not: Isaacson provides insight into Einstein's family and background:

> Einstein was descended, on both parents' sides, from Jewish tradesmen and peddlers who had, for at least two centuries, made modest livings in the rural villages of Swabia Southwestern Germany.

> He was blessed by being born into an independent-minded and intelligent family line that valued education, and his life was certainly affected, in ways both beautiful and tragic, by membership in a religious heritage that had a distinctive intellectual tradition and a history of being both outsiders and wonderers.

> Einstein's father, Hermann, was born in 1847 in the Swabian village of Buchau, whose thriving Jewish community was just beginning to enjoy the right to practice any vocation. Herman showed "a marked inclination for mathematics," ....

> .... [H]is docility did make him well suited to be a genial family man and good husband to a strong-willed woman. At age 29, he married Pauline Koch, eleven years his junior.

Pauline's father, Julius Koch, had built a considerable fortune as a grain dealer and purveyor to the royal Württemberg court.

Pauline and Hermann had a second and final child, a daughter, in November 1881, who was named Maria but throughout her life used instead the diminutive Maja. [...] Despite a few childhood squabbles, Maja was to become her brother's most intimate soul mate.

Based on the educational background and financial resources of Mr. Albert Einstein's parents, he seemingly had a relatively secure base to launch his childhood and cultivate the Genius within:

> [Einstein] was generally a loner, a tendency he claimed to cherish throughout his life, although his was a special sort of detachment that was interwoven with a relish for camaraderie and intellectual companionship. "From the very beginning he was inclined to separate himself from children his own age and to engage in daydreaming and meditative musing...."

> .... [A]s a young child, [Einstein was] prone to temper tantrums. [...] .... [H]e eventually outgrew his temper.

"Among the children at the elementary school, anti-Semitism was prevalent," he recalled.

Being taunted on his walks to and from school based on "racial characteristics about which the children were strangely aware" helped reinforce the sense of being an outsider, which would stay with him his entire life.

I'm not a psychologist by any stretch. However, I wonder to what degree Einstein's apparent "temper" was simply a reflection, an inartful exercise of his strong will. To what extent was his temperament, his strong will, his unique form of what some may describe as an introversion attribute, misunderstood? To develop into the trailblazer, intellectual, thought-leader that Mr. Einstein became, it's not difficult to appreciate how these attributes evolved into hallmarks of his genius or Genius. Furthermore, he also seemed to proverbially "turn lemon into lemonade" with respect to the anti-Semitism he encountered as a child. The taunting seemed to only stiffen his already unflappable, leather-textured-skin. If you and I walked seven miles in Mr. Einstein's shoes or walked seven miles barefoot through the terrain he encountered during that point in his childhood, depending on our own level of resiliency, would we also develop highly resistant Kevlar skin as he had? The poetry in motion is not only captured in the numerous achievements earned at the pinnacle of his life. More importantly, the poetry in motion is equally conspicuous throughout the course of HIS JOURNEY! The same sentiment also rings true in your life and throughout the course of YOUR JOURNEY:

> When he turned 9, Einstein moved up to a high school near the center of Munich, the Luitpold Gymnasium... known as an enlightened institution that emphasized math and science as well Latin and Greek. In addition, the school supplied a teacher to provide religious instruction for him and other Jews.

By age 12, his sister recalled, "he already had a pre-
dilection for solving complicated problems in applied
arithmetic," and he decided to see if he could jump
ahead by learning geometry and algebra on his own.
His parents bought him textbooks in advance so that
he could master them over summer vacation. [...] "Play
and playmates were forgotten," .... "For days on end
he sat alone, immersed in the search for a solution, not
giving up before he had found it."

His uncle Jakob Einstein, the engineer, introduced him
to the joys of algebra.

Einstein's greatest intellectual stimulation came from a
poor medical student who used to dine with his family
once a week. [...] His name was Max Talmud... and
he began his weekly visits when he was 21 and Einstein
was 10.

Talmud brought him science books, including a pop-
ular illustrated series called *People's Books on Natural
Science....* The twenty-one little volumes were written
by Aaron Bernstein, who stressed the interrelations
between biology and physics....

Judging from the thought experiments that Einstein
later used in creating his theory of relativity, Bernstein's
books appear to have been influential.

Talmud also helped Einstein continue to explore the
wonders of mathematics by giving him a textbook on
geometry years before he was scheduled to learn that
subject in school.

When Talmud arrived each Thursday, Einstein delight-
ed in showing him the problems he had solved that
week. Initially, Talmud was able to help him, but he
was soon surpassed by his pupil.

So the awed medical student moved on to introducing
Einstein to philosophy."

To his credit, Mr. Einstein demonstrated laser focus and
possessed an insatiable appetite when endeavoring to
digest the fruits of knowledge associated with mathematical postulates, theorems, and principles. His mind as a
youngster was without doubt very impressive. The schools
he attended, the quality of instruction he received, the
guidance he received from highly-educated relatives, and
the tutelage he received from his mentor (Max Talmud)
had all the trappings for accelerated intellectual and cognitive growth.

In contrast to Mr. Einstein, the environment and
training ground that existed during the childhood of Mr.
Christopher Langan appeared to be just the antithesis.
Outliers captures Langan's experience well:

> Chris Langan's mother was from San Francisco and
> was estranged from her family. She had four sons, each
> with a different father. Chris was the eldest. His father
> disappeared before Chris was born.... [...] Her fourth
> [husband] was a jailed journalist named Jack Langan.

Chris did not have a stable family setting. Furthermore, his
childhood would prove to be quite tumultuous. According
to Chris:

"To this day I haven't met anybody who was as poor when they were kids as our family was...." [...] I remember my brothers and I going into the bathroom and using the bathtub to wash our only set of clothes and we were bare-assed naked when we were doing that because we didn't have anything to wear."

One summer the family lived on an Indian reservation in a teepee, subsisting on government surplus peanut butter and cornmeal."

Growing up in a poor household and in an underprivileged community are experiences many of us can relate to:

Jack Langan would go on drinking sprees and disappear. [...] He used a bullwhip to keep the boys in line.

When the boys were in grade school, the family moved to Bozeman, Montana. One of Chris's brothers spent time in a foster home.

[At that point in time,] ".... Bozeman was a small hick town when we were growing up.

Yes; Chris Langan is the person "many call the smartest man in America." He is also the man whose IQ is estimated to be 195, which is 45 rungs above Albert Einstein's evaluated IQ of 150. That said, like everyone else, Chris and his family had to navigate through the bumpy, practical terrain of everyday life. The everyday terrain included practical needs such as finding stable shelter, finding temporary relief from the stresses of making a living to put food on the table and clothes on the children's back, Jack

Langan's drinking, dealing with divorce and other challenges associated with step parenting.

Chris received full scholarship offers from Reed College in Oregon and the University of Chicago after high school graduation. After choosing Reed College, Mr. Langan recalled:

> I had a real case of culture shock. I was a crew-cut kid... working as a ranch hand in the summers in Montana, and there I was, with a whole bunch of long-haired city kids, most of them from New York.

Ultimately, Chris lost his scholarship. This unfortunate predicament was due to his mom's failure to complete financial statements for the renewal of his scholarship.

In real time, sometimes we may not be able to appreciate all there is to admire about each other and ourselves, considering how lightning-quick time and space can feel as if it's moving. Sometimes only hindsight sprouts the appropriate level of perspective. I suspect that is a part of being human. At the conclusion of my research for this book, I was equally fascinated, gained an equal level of appreciation and depth of admiration for the unique Genius embodied in Albert Einstein and Christopher Langan, respectively. It would be a disservice for me to not have recognized how equally beautiful their minds were (are). Their respective journeys were (are) *perfectly imperfect*, which is no different from the once-in-a-lifetime journey you and I are in the midst of.

W. Clement Stone said "Aim for the moon. If you miss, you may hit a star." We often begin as children who dream big, set lofty goals, and aspire to voyage as far as our underdeveloped mind can think to reach. Many tangible and intangible variables inform, shape the nature of those dreams, goals, and aspirations. We mature into young adults then adults who eventually further embark into the world coliseum as if it were the Flavian Amphitheatre. The world coliseum brims with other *gladiators (your neighbors and everyday fellow human beings), Life Athletes (LA)* so to speak. The primary goal is to maximize and offer our innate talents and abilities to the world around us. Describing people as gladiators, or Life Athletes (LA), may seem like an exaggeration, however, isn't it apropos considering the myriad challenges (fights) and hurdles we all face throughout our lives? Meeting those challenges, rising to those occasions, and surmounting those hurdles require the durability, the perseverance, the warrior mentality of a gladiator. Exceeding expectations, moving forward when circumstances justify retreat, and following through with deep study, disciplined training, and thoughtful preparation require the focus, the endurance, the immersion of a Life Athlete (LA) (coined by yours truly).

Think of your own journey; compare, contrast how you initially envisioned your life would unfold to how your life ultimately unfolded or is unfolding. Think of how your innocent, youthful mind thought versus your now more experienced, mature mind. If you are a young person reading this book, understand the perspective from which the preceding sentences speak from. Our lives unfold *perfectly imperfect.* The journey from beginning to end for each of us is non-linear, replete with unanticipated turns, bends, and changes in direction. Some of our most memorable "victories" leave us with momentous awards, trophies and adulation, while some of our most damaging "defeats" or "mistakes" leave enormous scars, deep lacerations on our confidence and within our spirit. Certain junctures of our journey may seem uneventful, quiet, maybe akin to moving in slow motion, while other times seem to move feverishly at warp speed with tumult. While people may differ on which noun, verb or adjective they choose to describe these types of experiences, it's all a part of the universal *perfectly imperfect learning process (curve)* and training ground associated with being a human being.

What does *perfectly imperfect* mean within the context of this Amendment? Our respective journeys do not unfold with neat, ribbon-tied and gift wrapped, perfect outcomes, even when we may accomplish the goal we envisioned from the outset. There was nothing neither neat nor anything perfect about the anti-Semitism and taunting Einstein faced during his childhood. There was nothing idyllic about the domestic violence Mr. Langan, his siblings and his mom endured during his early years from his stepdad. Langan's domestic life was a mess. Neither was there anything neat nor perfect about the fact that his once in a lifetime intellect and potential went virtually underappreciated at educational institutions he stepped foot in. We encounter imprecise moments for which we employ ad hoc, improvisational responses (even when we prepared in advanced). At times, we may employ focused responses sourced from impressive stretches of individual (or collective) imagination and creativity. Other times, we react in a knee-jerk manner vice in more thoughtful ways. In essence, we react and we are *perfectly imperfect.*

Posited as a hypothetical, what if we surgically removed Einstein and Langan from the environments and realities of their respective biographies, swapping their immediate family, living conditions, and circumstances to be that of the other? What if Einstein was born into the same utter poverty, faced the same domestic abuse, and received the same level of indifference toward his intellect from the educational institutions he attended as Langan did? What if Langan was born from well-educated parents and relatives who valued education, attended quality educational institutions, and had the same opportunities as Einstein? What would their final respective outcomes look like? To what degree would their hypothetical outcome be similar or the antithesis of their real life? How would each handle the other's reality? Would the trajectory of Einstein's life still have positioned him to win the Nobel Peace Prize? Would Langan have won the Nobel Peace Prize in an area he was immensely passionate about as Einstein did? Would Einstein still have undergone or have accessed the institutional education rigor that facilitated the cultivation of insights, theories, and discoveries he made in theoretical physics? Would the trajectory of Langan's life have been better positioned to contribute his *Genius*, his unique *fingerprint* to a larger degree and on a grander scale? How would access to a more robust and comprehensive institutional education experience have even further buttressed an already unflinching intellect? My answer to those questions—I don't know! No one can answer these questions with any certainty, but we can make practical speculations.

We are products influenced by many different elements; many different elements influence the products (people) we are and become. Any change in the elements that influence us, even a scintilla of change to any degree, will produce a different version, different iteration of ourselves. If Einstein was born into the same utter poverty and faced the same domestic abuse as Chris Lagan, and if Langan was born from well-educated parents and relatives who valued education, then the resulting reel of their lives would show the ripple effect, visually looking different, coupled with different dynamics and outcomes. If Talmud had not brought Einstein science books to read and had not helped Einstein explore mathematics years before he would learn those subjects in school, who knows what the ripple effect would have been on not only his life, but also on humanity. However, there would have been some tangible effect. If certain experiences in your life and my life did not happen as they did, the aforementioned rings true also.

Albert Einstein's unique journey—similar to your journey and mine—which was shaped by his personal passion (i.e., intrinsic love of physics), environment, family, culture, life experiences, and a plethora of other elements, and his *perfectly imperfect* synthesis of those elements, coupled with his unique genetics, unique personality traits, and unique ability, cannot be replicated. The same can be said about

Christopher Langan; the same can be said about you and me. People may encounter similar conditions, similar challenges, similar experiences, have similar skill sets, similar passions, similar abilities, but no one can replicate another's exact journey. Therefore, the results, even in the most similar of situations, will still be dissimilar.

Some of those reasons are precisely why the book *Outliers* was so fascinating to me. *Outliers* pulled back the curtain, so to speak, displaying the steps that often take place, what *elements* often influence, what *elements* often exist before some of the most extraordinary, *perfectly imperfect* success stories occur. Illuminating to me was Mr. Gladwell's account of the social prestige, seemingly unending resources and access to privilege Mr. Robert Oppenheimer had the good fortune of being born into—how those tangible and intangible elements ultimately influenced the trajectory of his life and how the influence of those elements catapulted him to a life of great achievements. Juxtapose Mr. Oppenheimer next to self-taught Mr. Christopher Langan's tenacious, insatiable appetite to learn, building an unquestionable muscular intellect, despite having a sub-zero level of social prestige, scant resources and having been reared in a conspicuously underprivileged household.

Considering the heightened level of awareness of what *elements* influence success and our general collective understanding of this area of focus, adeptly discussed by Mr. Gladwell, what practical good can we do with that awareness? How can we use that awareness and understanding to manually engineer, in practical terms, more frequent success stories? I understand "success" is a subjective term. For all intents and purposes, my definition of success is not wedded to the monetary definition some may ascribe to success. Success from my vantage point is developing your mind, our minds to the point at which you (we) have the ability to contribute a mature form of your talent, your unique fingerprint, your unique Genius.

In Amendment 1 (*Infinite Human Potential, Part 1*) of this book, I put forth the question of how do we replicate the same formula for brilliance and *Genius* we see in Robert J. Anderson, as he plays the role of Little George in the movie *It's a Wonderful Life*? More specifically, how do we replicate that same formula for brilliance and *Genius* in every adult and child alike? As time passed between writing Amendment 1 and this current Amendment, my perspective changed on that question. The aim should not be to replicate the same formula for brilliance and Genius. Developing brilliance and Genius does not take one formula or a single approach; it can be done in various ways. Furthermore, what may have worked in Anderson's case may not necessarily work in your case or mine. The resources available to Anderson or the skill set he possessed are different from yours. Your raw attributes may require a different kind of cultivation and a different set of resources; if resources are not readily available, you may need a little more creativity and self-determination to forge through life challenges and obstacles throughout your journey. What is of the utmost importance with respect to your Genius is finding a way to share it, regardless of circumstance.

Who had the better mind between Einstein and Langan? Neither mind was better than the other, nor are their minds better than ours. Mr. Einsten's and Mr. Langan's respective stories are *different*—containing their own unique irony; presenting their own unique challenges and adversities; and having their own unique beauty and poetry intricately interwoven within the tapestry of their journey. If given an opportunity, under the right set of circumstances, for all of us, the sky is not the limit, but only the beginning, and our potentials are infinite. At times, our lack of understanding of how highly adaptive and incredible the human mind is, our lack of awareness of our latent potential that lurks beneath the surface or consciousness, or simple lack of belief in ourselves may decelerate how quickly we mature our Genius. The aforementioned is not a criticism of you (us). It is an endeavor to catalytically create more awareness. Every letter of every word throughout the pages of this book also applies to me or has applied to me at some point in my life. Fortunately, neither the present nor the past necessarily determine our futures.

AMENDMENT IV

Pathfinder

"I[, WE] WILL EITHER FIND A WAY,
OR MAKE ONE."

—HANNIBAL

With its genesis born in _humility_, its altruistic ending replete with _boundless hope_, this book seeks to encourage thinking anew about how we approach educating our children, educating ourselves, educating people in general, and finding practical, more creative approaches to better hone and maximize the unlimited potential of *every* human being. In that spirit, rhetorically, do our educational institutions and their instructors successfully tap into the endless creativity, imagination, and potential gold mines *all* of our children and adults have to offer? Do employers successfully cultivate and harvest the best employees have to offer; not only the most obvious, surface level skills, but the dormant talents that lay beneath? I suspect that some institutions and its instructors are more successful than others for a multitude of reasons. The same could be said for employers. There are a whole host of approaches to measuring success. Additionally challenging, we each may have varied definitions of success. In the traditional sense that I think of success, it means achieving a desired end goal. There are no simple and short answer to those questions. I don't purport to have or know the full answers. However, my perspectives will inform and galvanize efforts to assist in finding more effective solutions.

Development of the human mind is a process that takes place over time. From birth, every aspect of a child's environment contributes to his/her development (i.e., neuroplasticity); changes continually take place consciously and subconsciously. A child's mind is perpetually morphing, organizing and reorganizing as it undergoes neuroplasticity. In Amendment 2, the concept of neuroplasticity was briefly discussed. Beginning as early in your childhood as you can remember, think about your own intellectual development and growth. How did your environments shape your language and ability to communicate and mold your ability to think and make sense of the world?

We live in an imperfect world. In a perfect world, we *all* have perfect parents who provide the perfect tutelage, perfect peers who provide only perfect influence, perfect home and school environments conducive to accelerated learning, perfect instructors and mentors that mold us based on perfectly tailored approaches, and perfect conditions to cultivate self-direction/self-awareness/self-exploration/self-discovery/self-expansion (e.g., intellectually, physically, emotionally)/self-development. Access to all the aforementioned, though ideal, generally is not available to each and every one of us. By no means is that a new discovery; it's pretty common knowledge. You have likely seen countless news stories, are aware of countless books, venturing to offer insights, different angles, and windows into those themes and topics.

Our world requires us to successfully manage the deck of cards life deals to us, respectively, and to face the realities and adversities life presents head on with unwavering grit and dogged tenacity. The quote "I will either find a way, or make one" is attributed to Hannibal. In *General Hannibal Was One of the Most Creative Military Strategist in History* from National Geographic, Kristin Baird Rattini writes:

> Hannibal…set out to defeat Rome in the Second Punic War, beginning in 218 B.C. […] [His] daring advance through the Alps with at least 40,000 troops—and dozens of elephants—became legendary. The treacherous mountain conditions decimated his army to nearly half its size. The elephants, though, functioned as tanks do today, using their bulk to smash through enemy lines.

If my recollection serves me well, during my freshman year in high school, we covered the Punic Carthaginian military commander Hannibal in History class. At that time, I do not believe I had gained the proper level of appreciation for his Genius in the realm of military leadership. When discussing great military strategists in history from an accomplishment perspective, Hannibal's name is often mentioned together with Alexander the Great, Julius Caesar and others. Hannibal's reference, "I will either find a way, or make one," is a fitting mantra that encapsulates an inspirational figure that dredged her own way, used her

Genius to ax obstacles, clearing her own path—a "PATH-FINDER" of sorts. There are several lessons we can glean from this phenomenal woman. Keep reading, and I'll tell you more about her.

path- fin-der *noun or adjective* \ **path-ˌfīn-dir**

1—one that discovers a way; especially: one that explores untraversed regions to mark out a new route

2—a person who goes ahead of a group and finds the best way to travel through an unknown area

3—a person or group that is the first to do something and that makes it possible for others to do the same thing

Becoming "the first" person to do anything of far reaching historical and cultural significance is quite a feat. Regardless of which city, state or country you're from, history provides names of many who have been the first in their respective field, vocation, or career of choice. When we proverbially place ourselves in their shoes, attempt to think about how it must have felt to navigate through the previously uncharted territory, muddy waters. Attempt to think about the level of deft, level of skill employed to be successful in their given endeavors. I'm sure it can be quite a humbling experience. The cliché "[e]asier said than done" holds true. Simply holding the thought of being the person who maneuvers through the different crucibles prior to accomplishing the given feat is a far easier task than the actual execution. We not only laud their given achievement;

we also acknowledge the inherent hardships associated with being "the first" and appropriately hold in high esteem the challenging journey they dared to trek while ultimately staking their claim.

The story [or stories] behind the story [or stories] of the everyday person—people like you and me—can be quite climatic, quite dramatic if told through the lens of perspective and context. We may sometimes feel our respective story is anticlimactic or downright boring, because it may be difficult to fully appreciate the personal obstacle course, gymnasium, or jungle used to propel us through the various stages (and varying levels within those stages) of our lives. The jungle and gymnasium metaphors are relatable from these perspectives. If you were dropped smack-dab in the middle of a jungle for a time, just as in our day-to-day lives, you would be forced to adapt quickly, fend for yourself, survive, and then ultimately thrive in that environment. Learning curves would exist; continuous challenges would persist. In a gymnasium, before we engage in extremely vigorous activities or sports, we are taught to first complete preparation exercises that stretch us, that lubricate the elasticity of our muscles and tendons to facilitate optimal performance and also to avoid injury. As we navigate through our personal jungle, our personal gymnasium, life is inherently unpredictable, dynamic, hovering with what can seem like countless potential storylines.

If and when you and I have the good fortune of attending the theatre to watch a musical, play, or maybe the ballet, much goes on pre-performance, backstage before and during the live event. As an audience member, we are exposed to the final production of months, sometimes years or even decades of hard work, perseverance, and dedication. A costly amount of sacrifice, sweat, and oftentimes tears are intertwined into the backstory of each performer. Also, add a few ounces of unbridled passion, laser focus, and deep-seated love for good measure. These elements are not necessarily present in every story. However, some or all of the aforementioned elements are present in many.

Think deeply about your journey. What happens during pre-performance, backstage, before you clash in hopes of conquering your personal Goliath, achieving your goal and objective, solidifying your success and triumph? At what point on the spectrum are you in the process of developing and navigating through the evolution of refining your unique talents, gifts (Genius), abilities? Who are the major characters, the important places, the critical junctures that encompass your main plot? How do (did) you handle the challenge(s), ranging from large to small? Do (did) you embrace the challenge(s)? Are (were) you successful? Some of the answers that help create the feel, texture, and backdrop of our personal story come in the responses to those questions, though, not all-inclusive.

There are plenty of stories of people you and I know, who we draw inspiration from. Before we spotlight your story or even maybe a small fraction of mine, consider this: the sky level view of someone becoming "the first" is oftentimes eventful, marked by interesting twists and turns, fascinating ebbs and flows. At that altitude, you may typically learn about the general high and lowlights and the end result. However, the ground level story behind the story is far more informative, miles more compelling, threefold more captivating. It provides context, color, texture, feel, environment, explanation, depth, and insight. Against that backdrop, the ground level story of Misty comes to mind.

On June 30, 2015, Ms. Misty Danielle Copeland "became the first African American woman to be promoted to principal dancer in ABT's 75-year history," which is historically and culturally significant. For the sake of context, the founding of American Ballet Theatre (ABT) was in 1939. I am not a ballet aficionado; however, I do consider myself to be someone who maintains a general ear to and eye on pop culture. For a time, when I thought of professional ballet in the United States, there was not one person of color that leapt to mind—one of many reasons Ms. Copeland's achievement is so significant, so remarkable. Before Misty, there were very few principal ballet dancers of color across the United States; she is now in many respects a household name. After her wide acclaim and success, seeing multiple principal ballet dancers of color under contract with ABT is the norm. Other principal dancers of color in the year 2020 include the likes of Stella Abrera, Herman Cornejo, and Hee Seo.

September 10th, 1982 proved to be a very consequential date—the date Ms. Copeland was born in Kansas City Missouri. She was raised in the San Pedro community in Los Angeles, California. Having read her compelling story in *Life in Motion: An Unlikely Ballerina*, I learned Misty moved around frequently during her childhood and later adolescence. While the youngest of four children from her mom's second marriage, Ms. Copeland also has two younger half-siblings. Misty stands approximately 5 ft 2 (157 cm) and has a very petite frame. If you've seen one of her interviews, she has quite an impressive bearing and her countenance is endlessly charming. As you would expect from a ballerina, her posture is always a perfectly positioned right angle, legs crossed in a bow (if seated), and hair neatly done. She has a chestnut brown complexion and communicates with a gentle, delicate tone (at least that's what's conveyed in my mind). However, don't make the foolish error of thinking beneath her lady-like mannerisms, under her sturdy, calm demeanor there isn't an amazingly powerful, undeniably strong, and uniquely bold, brave juggernaut. More specifically, it is not her size that gives reason to describe her as a juggernaut; it is her will to hurdle obstacle after obstacle to eventually become the *first* African American woman to be promoted to principal dancer in ABT's 75-year history that renders her a full-fledged juggernaut.

When did I first see Misty Copeland perform in person? On May 16, 2017, I saw Ms. Copeland at the Metropolitan Opera House in New York City. She performed in "Don Quixote." The Metropolitan Opera House is a part of the massive Lincoln Center for the Performing Arts. Her performance in a couple of words: brilliant and phenomenal. Her dance style and movements are precise as if done with a scalpel, elegant, cleanly executed, nothing short of poetry and grace in motion. I was genuinely enchanted by the level of skill, exactness, the ease that accompanied her performance. She had performed in Vienna, VA the summer before and had performed at The Kennedy Center in Washington, DC on occasion. However, I had always seemed to miss out on tickets, because of how quickly her shows sell out. I highly recommend you see her perform in person for yourself.

Let's backtrack. How did I first learn about Misty Copeland? Sometime between 2013 – 2014 is when I first saw the "I Will What I Want" campaign commercial by Under Armour, via YouTube,[1] spotlighting Ms. Copeland. It is an approximately 60 second feature. At the outset, Misty stands ruler straight; steadily in an on-pointe position; the contours and muscle fibers of her calves, legs, abs, arms are on display and indicative of how healthy she is and how well she takes personal care of herself. The exterior surface of her skin is comparable to artwork, not a scratch, tear, blemish in sight. From head to left elbow to fingertips to right elbow to head again forms an almost perfect diamond shape. She is wearing what appears to be dark violet Under Armour athletic wear (tank top and pure stretch cheeky bottom) and tan ballet slippers. A gray chair and pair of gray and white Under Armour women's shoes also appear in the bottom left corner. This opening scene takes place in an all-white room with traditional beige wall mounted double ballet bars. At the same time, a piano is playing a very slow, melancholy melody in the background. A very soft-spoken young female voice (Raiya Goodman) narrates in the background:

> Dear candidate. Thank you for your application to our ballet academy. Unfortunately, you have not been

---

[1] "Under Armour – Misty Copeland I Will What I Want." *YouTube*, 16 Sep 2016, www.youtube.com/watch?v=DeTyNnALV4c.

accepted. You lack the right feet, Achilles tendons, turnout, torso length, and bust. You have the wrong body for ballet. And at 13, you are too old to be considered.

The commercial then teleports Misty from the all-white room to what appears to be a dark, stage-lit theatre. What you experience in that moment as you're watching the commercial is not merely a figment of your imagination. The tempo of the background music hastens, which quite naturally elevates your heartbeat; the feeling is palpable. She is no longer standing still, but now is dancing in freestyle form, effortlessly showcasing grace in motion, dynamic movements, and offering a small peek, a glimpse into her unique artistry. The spot eventually ends—the last phrase on the screen before the commercial concludes: I WILL WHAT I WANT.

The I WILL WHAT I WANT Under Armour commercial with Misty Copeland was, by far, one of the most riveting and indelible commercials I have personally experienced. Using the word "experienced," instead of simply seen, is not an exaggeration—the commercial overflows with heart-poundingly raw emotion. The words narrated during the spot provide a piece of a larger story, which continues on to date. As of 2020, Misty is still a thriving performer. It would be difficult to find someone with an untainted heart who could not appreciate the endurance, the resiliency her story embodies.

Ms. Misty Copeland did a phenomenal job with authoring insight into her life story in *Life in Motion:*

An Unlikely Ballerina. As a child, Misty and her siblings often moved around from place to place at the direction of her mom. Misty described her unstable upbringing in her book as follows: "Our leaving was always like that— dramatic, hurried, and ragged." She loved her mom dearly and her mom genuinely loved her children. That said, Ms. Copeland's childhood endured several stormy marriages of her mom gone awry. Despite not having a consistent place to call home and being faced with the practical challenges that accompany that sort of predicament, the light, the glow that shined brightly from within Misty would never dim.

Misty, I learned, is a very relatable person; a person who could easily be a sister, close friend, or girl next door. She easily has one of the most affable personalities you will ever encounter. When we see, hear about, learn about icons or other luminaries, sometimes their personal stories are so vastly disparate than ours, drawing inspiration or feeling kinship with them can be a bit challenging. Conversely, when the silhouette of their personal challenges mirrors ours, the weight and heaviness of their personal difficulties, idiosyncrasies, or quirks equal ours, generating encouragement from them during the course of our own journeys comes more naturally. Feeling heartened by their examples, being moved to think and be proactive in our own lives by their perseverance occur more fluidly. Ms. Copeland describes herself:

"…. [Misty is] quiet, introverted, and happy to disappear within the clamor…."

She further writes, "I was a nervous child...unease, coupled with a perpetual quest for perfection, made my life harder than it needed to be.

I think I was born worried. There wasn't a day that I didn't feel some kind of anxiety.... [...] I was just nervous about life, period. I felt awkward, as if I didn't fit in anywhere, and I lived in constant fear of letting my mother down, or my teachers, or myself."

Coincidentally, like Misty, I am also an introvert, generally quiet, more than happy to remain out of the limelight. Chasing "perfection" was an exercise in futility that I engaged in routinely. Furthermore, I also realize my cycle of thinking—for a time—made my life harder than it needed to be.

Interestingly enough, when you see Misty in the I WILL WHAT I WANT Under Armour commercial, nervous and awkward are likely the last adjectives that jump to mind. More fitting adjectives would be poised and effortlessly graceful. Her story is a reminder of how irony has a way of intersecting itself in life. As cliché as it may sound, our beginning does not necessarily dictate our future, nor does it determine the path we must take or how our lives should end. The *desire* and *will* to live out one's full potential are force multipliers. Having that awareness is also *power* in and of itself.

What is the benefit of having firsthand accounts of Misty's experiences if we can't learn from her story! I'm glad, I'm sure our world is glad Misty did not yield to how she felt about not being good at anything. How we feel in those formative years is not necessarily the reality; if ever. The life of a child and then later adolescence through the years of puberty can be a whirlwind. I admire Ms. Copeland's awareness of how her mind was wired. Misty shared how arduously she worked to inculcate details of certain subjects in her brain.

As amazingly talented of a dancer as Misty is, it is her humanity that is the most heartwarming. Her willingness to describe an unvarnished view of herself, personality and otherwise, again, makes her relatable. In addition, knowing how much effort she had put forth to excel in her academics further humanizes her. In many cases, there is no substitute for raw, unadulterated hard work, regardless of talent and ability. Hard work and effort buttress a person's gift, their Einstein (*Genius*). According to Misty:

I didn't feel particularly good at anything when it came to school.

Many people felt that way in school or children feel that way now. Misty went on to explain:

[S]o instead I worked incredibly hard, going over equations, pronouns, and dates of Civil War battles until they were imprinted on my brain...it would not be until I found ballet in my teenage years that I would realize the true gift of my visual memory—the ability to see movement and quickly imitate it.

Without a canvas, there's no work area for an aspiring artist to learn, practice, then create a masterpiece. Without a field, there's no place for an aspiring athlete to develop, hone, then display his or her physical talents, and on and on and on. It is vitally important to actively seek opportunities to access the tools and set ourselves in places, in positions to do what our gift uniquely equips us to offer the world. Amelia Earhart needed an airfield and an aircraft. Martin Luther King Jr. could use any venue to wield his masterful oratory skill and cadence and project his unique and very moving voice. Michael Jordan needed a basketball and a basketball court. As she discovered her gift—simultaneously aware of her draw to the arena of ballet and how performing provided a canvas, a field, a platform for her to explore, hone, then showcase her unique prowess—Misty soon became an admirer of famed gymnast Nadia Comaneci (1976 Olympics). Although the floor exercises in gymnastics don't precisely equate to classical ballet movement and dance, similarities exist. Eventually, she would teach herself gymnastics, doing backbend walkovers and handstands. An innate element of Ms. Copeland's gift (Genius) was the natural elasticity of her arms and legs. Early on, Misty was well aware she "could instantly do moves that it might take others months to achieve."

Ms. Copeland's unique visual memory, ease with memorizing and imitating movement reminds me of a penetrating concept I learned from a book years ago:

.... [W]e live in two distinct worlds. There is a world... of material objects, events and other people. This world existed before you were born and, if all goes well, it will continue to exist after you have gone. There is another world that exists only because you exist: the world of your own private consciousness, feelings and sensations. The latter being an *internal world*, so to speak. It goes on to say:

Your world is one in which, as the psychologist R.D. Laing put it, there is only one set of footprints. Your world came into being when you were born and it will end when you die. We share the first world with other people: we share the second world with no one. Recognizing the difference between *your* world and *the* world marks an important stage in the development of personal identity.

The section of the book I'm referring to is "Living In Two Worlds" of chapter five "Knowing Your Mind." The title of the book is *Out of Our Minds: Learning to be Creative* by author Sir Ken Robinson.

As I read Misty's story, I had a camera flash of insight! A window into the many characteristics encompassing her *internal world*; the latter of the two worlds Sir Robinson describes. In her internal world, visual memory appears to be inextricable linked to the muscle memory employed for dance. When Misty views a dance movement, it very quickly becomes glued into her memory; stamped in her consciousness. Through repetition, long-term muscle memory appears to take hold much quicker for her than the average person. Furthermore, she has an intrinsically insatiable desire to be her best (perfect or near perfect) at what she applies herself to, which is a driver of her irrepressible spirit. Along with Ms. Copeland's love of music since early childhood, ballet proved to be an opportune place for her to share her world, share her gift (Genius).

Here is an additional example that further illustrates differences in each person's internal world. Have you ever seen wingsuit flying or the BASE Jumpers who perform it? Wingsuit flying carries inherent fatality risk. The *internal world*, the *internal brain circuitry* and *neural wiring*—how they see, feel, process high altitudes—of a BASE Jumper is different from someone who is afraid of heights and avoids risk. Coupled with a multitude of other characteristics, such as personality, experience, and life exposure to name a few, even within the community of BASE Jumpers, the internal world of each of them is unique.

What other factors make Misty, BASE Jumpers, and each of us unique? As he discusses the intricacies of consciousness and the human brain, Sir Ken Robinson explains, "…. [O]ur senses are limited. We do not see the world as it is but as our particular human senses present it to us [and our varying level of intelligence perceive]." You and I can look at the same object, hear the same information and ultimately have different visual experiences, intellectually process the information in different ways. We see the object and hear the information through the binoculars and through the eardrum of our respective internal world, which is unique from person to person. As such, every person has the freedom, potential, ability to create and then offer something completely different to the world around us. He continues, "[t]he nature of our senses determines our field of perception: what we are actually able to perceive and how. There is more to the world than meets the eye, or...our senses. We live in a rich sensory environment, surrounded by sights, sounds, smells, temperature and textures, but we perceive only some of it." The sensitivity volume of Ms. Copeland's visual perception seems to have been conspicuously turned up (above average) from birth. As such, the manner in which her mind's visual perception synthesizes movement set her apart at an early age.

Another aspect of Misty's improbable story is the insertion of two very important figures who would become nurturers and mentors. The names of the two people are Elizabeth Cantine and Cynthia Bradley (Cindy). Elizabeth Cantine was Ms. Copeland's drill team coach at Dana Middle School in San Pedro, California. Ms. Cantine eventually introduced Misty to Cindy, which ultimately lead to her taking up ballet at the San Pedro Dance Center. Cindy also studied ballet during her childhood before succumbing to an injury that short circuited her career just prior to takeoff. Ms. Copeland was 13 years old at the time she met Cindy.

The value added contributed by her mentors is sincerely acknowledged in Misty's book, *Life in Motion*. The presence of a mentor, their tailored tutelage, keen insight, unique experience can have an invaluable influence on a person's life. Regardless of the career field, having the right mentor can accelerate one's growth and development far more rapidly than if she/he were not there. In Misty's case, Ms. Cantine and Cindy proved to be precisely who she needed in her life at those pivotal moments to keep her talents, her gifts (Genius), her trajectory moving forward in a positive direction. It may have been a different story if Ms. Cantine, Cindy, other significant figures and events had not shown up when they did or happen as they did. We have an extraordinary success story in Ms. Copeland.

If you are in a position to be a mentor and can give your time, expertise, wisdom to someone in need, I implore you to do so. In some cases, you may be the linchpin to a person realizing a dream, fulfilling a destiny, reaching their full potential. You will be hard pressed to find a more satisfying intrinsic reward than the feeling of having their genuine gratitude and appreciation. Undoubtedly, *I will* take my own advice as well.

In describing exchanges with one of her mentors, Misty shared:

Cindy said in all her years of dancing, in all her years of teaching, she had never seen anyone quite like me.

I'm not sure I believed her. But her praise piqued my curiosity....

When there is genuine rapport, trust, respect in a mentor/mentee relationship, the landscape becomes ripe for high levels of positive influence, encouragement, inspiration. In some instances, the mentee can surf on the wave of the mentor's deep-seated *belief* in them until the mentee develops an equal or superseding level of belief in themselves. Early on, Cindy could see potential in Misty that her fledgling mind and limited experience base at the time could not see yet. Cindy's uplifting words suffused the bones, muscle fibers in Misty's body and fed the fire, poured gas on the flame that already existed within.

Being a minority in an artform not traditionally performed by people of color, quite naturally, Misty carried that awareness with her. Having a mentor such as Cindy, who was not only equally aware of that reality, but also appeared to have proactively sought to counter that narrative, was a blessing. As Misty continued on, she notes:

> My classmates were mostly white, but there were a few other children of color.
>
> .... for a while it was we three brown kids, and our presence reflected Cindy's character and vision. She was different from most people in the ballet world, who felt Giselle and Odette were best performed by dovelike sprites, lissome and ivory-skinned. Cindy believed that ballet was richer when it embraced diverse shapes and colors. There would be times in my career when I would struggle to remember that, but I would eventually come back to that conviction, that the stage on which I performed was brighter for having me, even if some in the audience or dancing beside me didn't always agree.

As a mentee, one looks to the mentor to help mold them into a form above and beyond what she/he could do by themselves. It is a trusted responsibility never to be taken for granted. It was obvious Misty valued Cindy's approach to guiding her evolution:

> Cindy pushed me from the very start, putting me in an advanced class to see if I could keep up with students

who had been training for years. I could, and I did. That was a sign for her to push me even further and faster. Techniques that would normally take a young dancer months, even years, to learn, let alone perfect, I mastered in minutes.

Misty innately was already a person that enjoyed applying herself to be her very best; that attribute was (is) embedded in her DNA. Cindy, therefore, was a great match for her.

Saying "words matter" is very much a cliché. It may also sound simple. However simple it sounds, it is profoundly very true! Words can give life or death, can inspire or demotivate, can brighten up a day or bring gloom and doom. The end of chapter two, *Life in Motion*, etched a smile into my face when I read Misty's closing, as she summarizes her thoughts:

> I think that from the beginning, in her [Cindy's] mind, in her plan, stardom was my destiny....
>
> "The perfect ballerina has a small head, sloping shoulders, long legs, big feet, and a narrow rib cage," Cindy said one afternoon....
>
> She looked up and stared at me, adoringly. "That's you," she said softly. "You're perfect."
>
> I beamed.
>
> "You're going to dance in front of kings and queens," she said. "You will have a life most people cannot even imagine."

I began to believe her.

Cindy's perspective regarding Misty's physical attributes was the antithesis of the perspective laid out on the rejection letter read in the I WILL WHAT I WANT Under Armour commercial featuring Ms. Copeland— based on Misty's achievements, considering her accolades and highly decorated career, Cindy's assessment hit the bullseye.

We understand there is no such thing as "perfection" when endeavoring to serve as a mentor. While no one template works every time or for everyone, there are some universal principles, generally speaking, that prove quite beneficial during the course of a mentor/mentee relationship. The *belief* Cindy transfused into Misty coupled with Misty's own internal will, passion, drive, focus, and *growing belief* in her unique gift (Genius) is an example of the inner workings of an effective mentor/mentee paradigm. Rudimentary approaches such as right-sizing challenges and the degree to which a mentor pushes the mentee to reach beyond self-perceived and self-imposed boundaries, tailoring communication and continuous feedback, being a source of inspiration who nurtures hopes and dreams can create an environment for the mentee to thrive, to flourish, to eventually reach for the stars or perhaps another galaxy, and fly on their own!

Misty Copeland "became the first African American woman to be promoted to principal dancer in ABT's 75-year history," on June 30, 2015. ABT, New York City Ballet, and San Francisco Ballet are the three most prestigious United States classical ballet companies. It is important to note there were other African Americans who preceded Misty in making ballet history *outside ABT*, such as Raven Wilkinson. After recently perusing a PBS article, I learned a little more about her. Ms. Wilkinson "was one of the first African American ballerinas permitted to join a ballet company. During the 1950s, she danced with the [European] Ballets Russes de Monte Carlo under the condition that she pose as a white woman by painting her face." Ms. Wilkinson would leave "Ballets Russes and eventually landed a spot in the Dutch National Ballet."

Misty Copeland is a bonafide *pathfinder*—ABT was untraversed territory before Misty; there were no other African Americans at ABT before her. Through years of perseverance, dedication, fine tuning, honing her craft, *she found a way for herself; she made a way for herself.* Backstage, behind the curtains, behind the scenes of her story, she had numerous challenges, multiple obstacles as I've described throughout this Amendment. Misty's book *Life in Motion* provides her beautiful story in more vivid detail.

During the natural course of her life, Misty Copeland exhibited tremendous heart, discipline, dogged determination, belief in herself and gift (Genius), which eventually paid dividends. Misty also had mentors along her journey to facilitate navigation through the challenges that would surface ahead of her. Through it all, all her many success, accomplishments, and the history she has made, Misty remains a humble, down-to-earth spirit—a universal inspiration.

It is also important to remember Misty is not only a Genius in how she performs ballet. Ballet is simply the one arena she has devoted the most time, attention, and deliberate concentration since childhood. Discussed in the preamble of this book, I have *redefined* Genius. Genius is portable and can be applied to those subject areas we so choose. Genius exists on a spectrum and is tied to the uniqueness of our internal world. Her Genius, as it applies to ballet, was in its incubation period when she was a child; it has grown, matured over the years. If she chooses, regardless of whether it is right or left brain driven, she has the ability to apply her Genius to business, science, a vocation, or in other arenas. In part, the level of intrinsic excitement, stimulation, interest, and passion associated with what she applies her Genius to correspondingly influence how expeditiously the Genius develops in that realm, to what degree it grows and matures. At that point, her Genius would again be in an incubation period and grow as she grows in her studies. The spectrum, progression, and process of maturity are the same for us all. Misty did not become a Genius after her phenomenal accomplishments. She was born a Genius. Einstein did not become a Genius after he won the Nobel Prize in Physics in 1922. He was born a Genius. Again, his Genius was in its incubation period when he was a child; it grew, matured over the years. Just as the example with Misty, he could have applied his Genius (gifts) to business, a vocation, or in other arenas. The same is true for you. You were born a Genius. It is up to *you*, it's up to *us* to grow it, to mature it.

In Misty Copeland's *internal world*, her visual memory set her apart from her peers. The by-product of her unique visual memory is a marvelous wizardry of movement. It allows her to synthesize motion, learn complex choreography, execute dance routines far quicker than most. What about you? What specifically sets you apart? What is unique about the infrastructure of *your internal world*? Is it the unique sensitivity of your ears and fingers to hear and play heartfelt music? Is it the unique ability of your mind to dissect information, communicate effectively, and inspire in politics? Is it the unique angle of your thought and wonder to challenge existing phenomena and explore and discover in science? Is it the unique mental algorithms to create your own equation in math or logic in technology? Is it the unique way of using your imagination and song to craft delightful, resonant lyrical content? Is it your unique and uncanny ability to generate novel and innovative ideas to engine entrepreneurship? Is it your unique way of motivating and connecting with the human heart? Is it your uniquely mesmerizing elocution as a speaker? Is it your uniquely bedazzling, enthralling writing style? Is it your unique medley of ingredients, flavors, and textures as a chef? Is it your unique photographic memory to recall court cases, decisions, laws to bury the opposing prosecution or defense? Is it your unique approach to education and educating children? It's up to you to know what *it is* and what *it can become*. **As Sir Ken Robinson discussed in his book, the colors, textures, beauty, poetry, thoughts, science, etc., of your *internal world* are unique to you and no one else—only you can share it with the rest of**

us! I encourage you to please find a way to do so; make a way if you must!

Have you carved out time to take inventory of your gift(s) (Genius)? Misty was fortunate during her exploration of dance and then ballet to discover her "true gift," her Genius. How early did you discover your gift(s) (Genius), or have you discovered it or discovered them at all? In Ms. Copeland's case, her *potential* was given an opportunity to be unearthed, challenged, maximized. She had an internal gold mine, which we all possess in some unique form, but it had to be tapped into.

How do we ensure a success story like Misty Copeland's becomes the norm rather than the exception? The next seconds, the next moments, the next days, the next years, coupled with the choices we make (and other factors) along our journeys determine our futures. The Hannibal quote at the beginning of Amendment IV, "I[, we] will either find a way, or make one," is also a fitting segue to introduce the "Transition Person" term coined by Mr. Stephen R. Covey and expound on its relevancy to overarching ideas touched on thus far. Covey explained the Transition Person term in his book titled *The 7 Habits of Highly Effective People.* You and I also have the ability to be a Transition Person.

AMENDMENT V

Transition
Person

"IF THERE IS EVEN A FRACTION OF A
SECOND...THAT SPACE REPRESENTS OUR
POWER TO CHOOSE...."

—STEPHEN R. COVEY

As cited in Amendment III, Mr. Chris Langan, who is not widely known for his work, had an IQ of 195, 45 rungs above Mr. Einstein. Yet, Mr. Langan's accomplishments and achievements are nowhere close to what he envisioned for himself. Despite a rarified high IQ, some may say he never achieved anything commensurate with the level of his vast, immeasurable potential.

If Mr. Langan's educational institutions and teachers/professors throughout his life viewed and understood him to be a Genius from the outset, I wonder to what degree his life and worldly contributions would be different. Would they have sought to intentionally be more helpful to Langan's journey or consciously put him in environments that would best serve as a platform for his Genius to flourish and potentially serve the masses? If every human being is viewed and understood to be a Genius from birth, to what degree would our lives and worldly contributions be significantly enhanced? The desire to answer those questions and also engineer that reality are, in large part, the drivers for this book.

It is also important to have interest in the Genius of others as we do our own. We should not only be passionate about developing, nurturing, and sharing our Genius, we should also be passionate about learning about the Genius of our fellow human beings (our neighbors) and what their respective Genius offers. It is more likely than not you may benefit from their Genius, knowledge, wisdom, and understanding—the opportunity to directly or indirectly synergize with them may be a possibility as well. At a minimum, if you don't personally benefit from the Genius of your fellow human being, we will. As an example, I've certainly benefited from the Genius in the form of ideas and thoughts originating from Mr. Stephen R. Covey.

The first time I heard the name Stephen R. Covey was when a co-worker recommended the book *The 7 Habits of Highly Effective People*, which I will refer to as 'The 7 Habits' for short. The popularity of The 7 Habits is very well known—truck loads of copies have sold worldwide. I personally learned a lot from The 7 Habits. Some consider it a self-help book rooted in timeless approaches and proven thought patterns (i.e., "habits") that translate into becoming an effective agent when pursuing goals. The sibling or continuation of The 7 Habits is the book *The 8th Habit, From Effectiveness to Greatness* [The 8th Habit].

Chapter four of The 8th Habit, which is titled "Discover Your Voice—Unopened Birth-Gifts," is when I first saw the term "Transition Person" and the accompanying definition given by Mr. Covey: "One who stops unworthy tendencies from being passed on from prior generations to those that follow (your children and grandchildren)."

Leading up to the definition of Transition Person, Mr. Covey contextualizes:

> "If there is even a fraction of a second between stimulus and response, that space represents our power to choose our response to any situation."

No matter what happens to us in life or the circumstances we find ourselves in, the choice of how we respond is in our hands; it's our choice. It may sound like a banal recycled platitude or some sort of positive thinking mantra, but it's true. Responses to life's curve balls may require more courage, more self-determination, more resiliency than others. Mr. Covey continued:

> "Certainly, there are things that happen to us over which we have no choice. One such thing would be our genetic makeup. Though we do not choose our genes, we do have the power to choose how we respond to them. If you have a genetic predisposition to a particular disease, that doesn't mean that you'll necessarily get the disease. By using that self-awareness and your willpower to follow a regimen of proper exercise and nutrition and the most advanced medical wisdom, you may avoid the very illnesses or cancers that have taken your ancestors."

Having read the "Transition Person" definition, having gained an understanding of its intent, I'm inspired by it. The definition has a certain redeeming quality, in that by choosing to be a "Transition Person," one retains the power to unlock the metaphorical handcuffs that bind them to unworthy tendencies that cause harm or distress. You, we possess the will and are the ultimate decision makers as to when we become free from any self or externally imposed mental incarceration.

Regardless of which continent you reside, people generally would like to leave the world (to future generations) in a better place than when they arrived. Mr. Covey reminds us that at various junctures throughout life, we have a series of choices that determine how our lives eventually play out. While certain events and choices may be out of our control, it is vitally important to maintain *self-awareness* of the events and choices in our control. Self-awareness can counter perceived inevitability of negative outcomes due to circumstances or powers out of one's control, and it facilitates a "Transition Person" mindset. Mr. Covey further illustrates his perspective by citing a quote from psychiatrist R.D. Laing that emphasizes the importance of self-awareness: "The range of what we think and do is limited by what we fail to notice. And because we fail to notice we fail to notice, there is little we can do to change; until we notice how failing to notice shapes our thoughts and deeds." As he continues, Mr. Covey states, "[a]n awareness of our freedom and power to choose is affirming because it can excite our sense of possibility and potential."

We can aim to be a "Transition Person" at any point in time if we choose to be. In Ms. Misty Copeland's case, she did not necessarily set out to be a "Transition Person." Ultimately, the contours and outcome of her story are what establish her as such. Dance, and then specifically ballet, are simply arenas she enjoys displaying her artistry. American Ballet Theatre (ABT) seemed to have had a tendency to disqualify dancers built like Misty. Misty's body type was more muscular than ABT had accepted for its principal dancers in the past. ABT's body type preference at that time, I suspect, was based on historical paradigms and preferences. As she progressed through her ballet career, eventually her talent and her Genius became undeniable. ABT was forced by Misty's grace and dynamism to redefine body type parameters for its principal dancers and also be more open to a wider variety of body shapes. Ms. Copeland is a source of inspiration to countless children and adults alike and will be a source of inspiration not only to future ABT prospects, but to future generations of dancers and non-dancers to come.

* * * *

It is far easier to laugh than attempt to make someone else laugh. I've heard it said laughter is not only good for the soul, it's also great for your health. When I laugh, the weight of life feels lighter. My core doesn't feel entangled in knots. Depending on the depth from which the particular laugh originates or what clever details made me laugh in the first place, any concern I may have had seems to bury itself somewhere in my subconscious, no longer preoccupying my mind with the options, decisions, or dynamics of a given issue at hand. I also learned "[l]aughter enhances your intake of oxygen-rich air, stimulates your heart, lungs and muscles, and increases the endorphins that are released by your brain."

There is an art to engendering the sort of quirky thinking, unconventional or unafraid thought-chain, and mind mechanics that lead to a genuine, visceral laugh. Like with many other aspects of life, different degrees of laughter and different kinds of laughter exist on a spectrum. Laughter that originates from what is minimally funny (surface level laughter) to the sort of deep belly-laugh at what is hysterically hilarious. One of my personal favorite comedians who specializes in engendering laughter is Jim Carrey.

You don't necessarily need to be a movie buff to have at least seen one of Mr. Carrey's movies. *Ace Ventura: When Nature Calls* and *The Cable Guy* are two on a long list of his enjoyable, ridiculously funny movies—at least in my world they are. Do either of those movies ring a bell? He has a unique gift, a unique Genius to make people laugh, including me. His brand of humor falls on the side of the spectrum that leads you to laugh uncontrollably at times. Additionally, he also typifies, in my mind, what it means to be a "Transition Person."

James (Jim) Eugene Carrey was born January 17, 1962 in Ontario, Canada. He later became a United States citizen through naturalization in 2004. On television or in movies, he generally looks like a towering giant next to his castmates (at least he did to me). In reality, he is more so a small giant at an impressive height of 6' 2". Jim has a very slender frame, which adds to the appearance of being very tall and wiry. His face, his facial expressions, his entire body and how he spastically contorts them and uses them to cultivate laughs are parts of Mr. Carrey's charm, repertoire, and very much elements of what make him so uniquely funny.

To understand why I view Jim Carrey as a "Transition Person," why I believe he is someone who, with intention, stopped unworthy tendencies from being passed on from prior generations to those that follow *by his example*, it's helpful to have more context about his family. His mom Kathleen was a homemaker and dad Percy was an accountant and jazz musician. In addition, ironically enough, his dad was also a comedian according to Jim. He and his family lived a modest lifestyle with limited means, and unfortunately, his dad Percy was let go from his accounting job when Jim was 12 years old:

> Carrey's early adolescence took a turn for the tragic, however, when the family was forced to relocate from their cozy town of Newmarket to Scarborough (a Toronto suburb). They all took security and janitorial jobs in the Titan Wheels factory, Jim working 8-hour shifts after school let out (not surprisingly, his grades and morale both suffered). When they finally deserted the factory, the family lived out of a Volkswagen camper van until they could return to Toronto.

Jim discussed nuggets of wisdom learned from his dad's experience in a very inspirational YouTube[2] post; the title

[2] "Jim Carrey – Lessons from my father." *YouTube*, 19 Nov 2017, www.youtube.com/watch?v=FSY-hDlx5yk.

of the post is "Jim Carrey – Lessons from my father." He is giving a college commencement speech, wearing a dark gold cap and gown. He's on the stage; graduating seniors and faculty are listening ever so closely to every word with bated breath. In this 12 minute/16 seconds long video clip, Jim begins by saying, "Now fear is going to be a player in your life, but you get to decide how much." He continues on, "So many of us choose our path out of fear disguised as practicality. What we really want seems impossibly out of reach and ridiculous to expect, so we never dare to ask the universe for it. I'm saying, I'm the proof you can ask the universe for it."

Whether as a verb (to be afraid of) or noun (unpleasant emotion caused by anticipation or awareness of danger), we understand how the "fear" Jim Carrey refers to can inhibit us from doing what we are most passionate about, and, in some cases, restrain us from either sharing our Genius and/ or accomplishing goals associated with our unique talents and Genius. Regardless of age, career field, or vocation, unless you've had the good fortune of not ever being bit by the fear bug, we can identify the role it plays in decision making throughout our lives. Fear is not always an impediment; it can also be a source of fuel to drive us faster, harder to fulfill our dreams and reach our full potential.

Jim continues, "My father could have been a great comedian, but he didn't believe that was possible for him. And so, he made a conservative choice. Instead, he got a safe job as an accountant. And when I was 12 years old, he was let go from that safe job, and our family had to do whatever we could to survive. I learned many great lessons from my father, not the least of which was that you can fail at what you don't want. So, you might as well take a chance at doing what you love."

Mr. Jim Carrey's deeply personal sentiments and wisdom gleaned from his father's journey and his own moved me (I encourage you to view the referenced YouTube clip and digest it for yourself). He saw firsthand his father's human shortcomings while growing up. Jim then, very consciously, made his own decision NOT to mirror the fear his dad had of following his dreams and sharing his Genius. Jim would not succumb to settling for the *practical decision*, the *practical life*, or the *practical journey*. He dared to *dream big*, to *imagine beyond* his immediate circumstances early on, to *reach as long and far* as his Genius could touch and take him.

I don't personally know Mr. Jim Carrey, but I suspect as he grew up, it would have been easier to adopt the more likely outlook of believing his dream was virtually impossible or out of reach. If he had done so, he would have followed in his father's footsteps, choosing the safe choice and "path of least resistance." However, Jim chose to be the one who decided the size and magnitude of his dreams; he refused to succumb to internal voices of fear. Life generally does not happen on a totally linear track; at least not that I've seen. Having that awareness can help when life sometime unfolds or takes a different trajectory than we initially envision. Along the journey, countless life lessons present themselves for us to grow from as we fine tune and sharpen our talents and Genius.

Mr. Carrey's journey from humble beginnings in Ontario, Canada to becoming an A-list actor in Hollywood, California is awe-inspiring. His shooting star did not reach its impressive height overnight. His Genius and talents would eventually be shared widely through television and movies because of intentional, deliberate hard work and perseverance. I remember reading a book that quoted Robert Schuller by saying, "Yard by yard, life is hard. But inch by inch, it's a cinch." The progression of life and the pursuit to share our Genius are not as easily guided by one quote or another; however, I personally found this quote very helpful along my own journey. Processing life, projects, goals, and endeavors in small, bite-size bits and pieces, in inches, vice yards, can be a helpful approach to achievement. If you prefer the yard by yard or mile by mile approach, do what works best for you.

Earlier in this Amendment, I shared Stephen Covey's thoughts on the influences and forces that differentiate a "Transition Person:" "If there is even a fraction of a second between stimulus and response, that space represents our power to choose our response to any situation." Mr. Jim Carrey's *chosen response* was to chart a course leading to a life that was antithetical to his father's life. As a result, though we weren't lucky enough to benefit from the comedy, talents, and Genius of his dad on a larger scale, we've been fortunate to witness and benefit from the Genius Jim Carrey has offered over the years and continues to offer. You, we have the same choice in how we respond to every aspect of life!

Jim's example, his deeds, and his words are a basis to prevent the *fear* (unworthy tendency) his father had from being passed on to his child, his child's child, and so on and so forth. He has only one child, and regardless of his child's journey and eventual outcome, Jim has done his part. For those reasons, Mr. Jim Carrey is truly a "Transition Person." Jim was not only fearless as a person, his brand of comedy was also uniquely fearless and, to our benefit, hysterically fun and belly funny.

Let's share our Genius; whatever your Genius is, leave a legacy you're proud of! There were a couple of other lines in Mr. Carrey's YouTube clip that further resonated with me. As he finished his speech, he said "[a]s someone who has done what you are about to go and do, I can tell you, the affect you have on others is the most valuable currency there is. Because everything you gain in life will rot and fall apart, and all that will be left of you, is what was in your heart." When stating "everything you gain in life will rot," I believe he means, in part, the *tangible things* you gain in life—this is an enormously valuable reminder. In my own personal life, I have not been someone who places a ton of value in tangible things. I place more value in people and relationships. My intention here is to further amplify the value in Jim's words, considering it is a priority of mine to encourage others to share their talents and Genius.

So, what about *intangible things?* Your Genius (*The Einstein Within*) doesn't literally gather dust, rust, rot, or fall apart, but it can be stifled or atrophy. For it to grow and mature, it needs to be mindfully developed, honed, nurtured, and maintained. Only then can the lasting affect you/we have on others be the most impactful. With respect to his mention of the affect you have on others being the most valuable currency, take a moment to think earnestly, think deeply about that. Which relationships and which of the fondest moments associated with those relationships have been the most influential, the most inspirational to molding you along your life, your journey? What affect, what effect did those relationships and people have on you (and maybe still have on you today)?

Mr. Jim Carrey's Genius did not commence when he became an A-list Hollywood actor/star/comedian. Jim's *Genius* was incubated within his innermost recesses at birth and continues to evolve today ('*non-stationary-force*'), being formed and shaped during every microsecond of his life. His outgoing personality, ability to do impersonations, range of acting from comedy to drama, his mental elasticity in mind and physical elasticity in body, ability to pull you and me into laughter, and angles on engendering laughs are some of the incredible components of his unique Genius. In that regard, Jim Carrey's Genius (*The Einstein Within*) is different, disparate, distinct, and similar at the same time to the respective Genius of Robert J. Anderson (Little George Bailey), Albert Einstein, Christopher Langan, Natalie Portman, and Misty Copeland—and also different, disparate, distinct, and similar to the respective Genius possessed by you and me.

AMENDMENT VI

The Einstein Within You!

"IMAGINATION IS MORE IMPORTANT
THAN KNOWLEDGE."

—ALBERT EINSTEIN

Use your Genius to *imagine* the world we live in differently in order to do, create, invent, expand on, and/or perform something *new* and then share it with us all! I'll take my own advice and do the same. Einstein's full quote states:

> I am enough of an artist to draw freely upon my imagination. Imagination is more important than knowledge. For knowledge is limited, whereas imagination encircles the world.

Each of us is an artist, a conductor, a maestro in our own right. As Einstein urges, "draw freely," pull freely from the infinite treasure chest that is your imagination. Your fusion of ideas, creative interconnections, trains of thought, and angle of perspectives through the lens of imagination have the potential to influence, change our world for the better.

In the preamble of this book, I underscored the fact that no two human beings have the same fingerprints; the same is true for identical twins. Regarding *The Einstein Within You* (i.e., *your Genius*), its architecture and internal workings are different for each of us. Genius is *manifested* by what and how you do, create, invent, expand, perform with your amalgam of unique attributes, resulting in what I term *"fingerprints."* Left dormant, slumbering from non-use or neglect, your Genius benefits no one. Your Genius comes to life when you bring everything that is unique about you and innate to you from inside out and manifest it in some form. I intentionally use the word *Einstein* to be a synonym for *Genius*, considering Einstein is universally thought of as the quintessential genius.

In the world of rap music, from my perspective, as an artist, you earn respect based on your ability to not only bring your unique style, sound, and perspective, but also based on your play on words (i.e., combination of word positioning, word selection, and word synthesis = wordplay). Marshall Bruce Mathers III, more widely known as Eminem, is a famous rap artist acclaimed for his lyrical dexterity and crafty wordplay. He has a very memorable song that was released in 2002 from the motion picture *8 Mile*. The name of the song is titled *Lose Yourself*; it was the lead single from the *8 Mile* soundtrack.

I personally enjoy what I describe as song subtlety. In my mind, my internal universe, I appreciate when a song begins slowly, adding and building sounds, melodies, instruments, and beats (sometimes one at a time) until the full instrumentation and rhythms are playing at the same time. That is a part of my multi-dimensional, multi-sensory music listening experience. My goal is to immerse myself, to lose myself in the music. There are times when I close my eyes, mentally dive into the pool of sound waves, absorb the organic feeling and texture of the sounds, emotions, and visuals they elicit, and allow the music listening experience to take its course. Needless to say, I take music listening seriously, but yet it's such fun and endlessly stimulating.

I remember when I first heard the song *Lose Yourself.* I was in my car, driving home from a long day's work. I was exhausted from an early morning shift that began at 4AM and continued through the afternoon, but it felt more like I had just ended a double shift. At that time in my life, I routinely woke up at 3AM to prepare for work, would quickly guzzle down something for breakfast, and then make it to work to begin my shift by 4AM. The radio is what I relied on to keep my mind preoccupied as I drove home to take my daily afterwork nap. The song begins with a guitar playing power chords—after hearing *Lose Yourself* the first time, that signature power chord intro is indelibly in your mind. The low pitch sound seems to touch the pit of your stomach. The rest of the instrumentation eventually settles in. Eminem then proceeds to devour the track with his vivid, almost tactile lyrics and wordplay on seizing the moment. *Lose Yourself* by Eminem went on to win multiple awards (not an all-inclusive list): Grammy for Best Male Rap Solo Performance, Grammy for Best Rap Song, Academy Award for Best Original Song, and Best Video from a Film in the 2003 MTV Video Music Awards (VMA).

The kind of immersion that is representative of what
Eminem referenced in his song *Lose Yourself* is the kind
of intense focus and dedication of self we try to apply to
activities that are important, have meaning, and have value.
The more we immerse or lose ourselves in a given activity,
the more likely we are to generate a fruitful outcome. To
lose ourselves is akin to the concept of "flow," which I read
about in Mihaly Csikszentmihalyi's book *Flow: The Psychology of Optimal Experience.*

Mr. Csikszentmihalyi, a Hungarian-American psychologist, is considered a leading expert on the topic of "flow."
After all, he is credited with naming the psychological concept of "flow." In his book *Flow: The Psychology of Optimal
Experience*, Csikszentmihalyi describes "flow" as "the process of total involvement with life." Mr. Csikszentmihalyi
"…. uses the term 'optimal experience' to describe those
occasions where we feel a sense of exhilaration, a deep sense
of enjoyment…." He developed the "…. theory of optimal
experience based on the concept *flow*—the state in which
people are so involved in an activity that nothing else seems
to matter; the experience itself is so enjoyable that people
will do it even at great cost, for the sheer sake of doing it."
If you've heard the sports metaphor that a person is in a
"zone," the space or place they are in, whether physically,
mentally, or a combination of both is analogous to "flow."
The article *Being In The Zone: The Flow State In Athletic
Endeavors* by Valerie Worthington provides a noteworthy
attempt to describe how it feels to be in an athletic zone.
Valerie describes being in a zone as a feeling of invincibility.
She writes:

A good visual example of it is in the movie *The Matrix*, specifically the scene where the character Neo is dodging bullets being shot at him. To Neo, the bullets appear to be moving in slow motion, enabling him to dodge them effortlessly, because he can see them coming far in advance and react in plenty of time.

One of the most famous examples of flow or being in a zone in American sports history is given to us by the most well-known and legendary National Basketball Association (NBA) player of all-time, Michael Jeffrey Jordan. Mr. Jordan is commonly referred to by his initials "MJ," "His Airness," or simply Jordan. For the sake of context, here are just a few of his accomplishments from a much longer laundry list: 11-time All-NBA, 9-time All-Defensive Team, 6-time NBA Finals Most Valuable Player, NBA Rookie of the Year, 5-time NBA Most Valuable Player, 2 Olympic Gold Medals, and 3 NBA All-Star Most Valuable Player. Needless to say, Jordan is an exceptional athlete and basketball player.

Like many kids who grew up during Jordan's NBA career with the Chicago Bulls, I had (and still have to this day) a huge appreciation and enormous respect for his basketball talent. His love and passion for the game of basketball, his intrepidness as a competitor, his relentless work ethic, his personal style of play on the court, his unyielding will to win are just a few attributes associated with Jordan's Genius. Every dominating jump he made with the intent of dunking the ball in the rim was a display of mastery in the air and nothing short of pure grace, technical skill, and beauty. On defense, Jordan was one of the best in the league. He was a thief on the court, often stealing his defender's ball or his teammate's unsuspecting defender's ball. On offense, he scored virtually at will, almost whenever, wherever, and however he chose. As a 3-point shooter, however, some may describe Jordan's ability as good to average. For the record, using the adjectives "good" and "average" to describe any other aspect of his game is unheard-of. According to NBA.com, Jordan's career 3-point average is 32.7%. That means he made just over three 3-point shots out of every 10 attempted. According to basketball-reference.com and bleachereport.com, the person with the all-time number 1 ranked career 3-point percent from the NBA is Steve Kerr at 45.4%. Having that understanding sets the stage for the playoff game that produced his famous "shoulder shrug" or "Shrug Game," which personified flow or being in a zone from a sports perspective.

The day was June 3rd, 1992. The matchup was the Portland Trailblazers vs. Chicago Bulls in Game 1 of the NBA Finals. My brother and I had front row seats to the game in our comfortable, yet modest bedroom, on our Magnavox cathode-ray tube (CRT) color television. We both enjoyed the sport and played on junior high and high school basketball teams. We looked forward to the NBA Finals yearly and had feverish anticipation of seeing the Chicago Bulls compete for another NBA Championship. I was a die-hard Bulls fan, while my brother's loyalty and affinity were wedded to the Los Angeles Lakers. In the previous year, the Bulls defeated the Lakers in a best of 7 series, 4 games to 1. As a consequence, my brother was rather bitter towards the Bulls and he was eager to root against them this time around. Our excitement pre-game and throughout the Game 1 dual was palpable.

I read an article by Aaron Dodson titled *On this day in NBA Finals history: Michael Jordan's 'Shrug Game'* that helped place Jordan's shoulder shrug moment that night in June 1992 in proper perspective:

.... [H]e was an absolute assassin from behind the arc. Jordan...dropped six deep balls [meaning 3-pointers] in the first half alone, tying a Finals record for 3s in a half, set by Michael Cooper in 1987 and tied by Bill Laimbeer in 1990 (Ray Allen broke the record in Game 2 of the 2010 Finals with seven first-half 3-pointers.)

"Shots started dropping from everywhere," said Jordan after Chicago's 122-89 win, which he finished with 39 points.... "I started running for the 3-point line. It felt like a free throw, really."

After connecting on his sixth 3-poniter of the night, which he swished over his defender Cliff Robinson, Jordan turned to the scorer's table and shook his head three times. Then, as he jogged back down the court, he employed a simple shrug of his shoulders.

This wasn't a Maximus Decimus Meridius [from the 2000 feature film Gladiator] "Are you not entertained?" moment. This was a humble "Yup, I can't believe it, either" reaction to his atypical 3-point shooting ability.

As my brother and I watched, we both realized and understood Jordan was in "flow;" he was in a zone. On that night, during that stretch, his attention, focus, eyes, hands and body coordination were so deeply immersed that his on and off 3-point shot became as undemanding to him as making a free throw. Although not at Chicago Stadium that night, we felt the adrenaline, the thrill of Jordan's six 3-pointers, followed by the famous shoulder shrug, through the television screen.

Existing in a state of flow or in a zone is not unique to athletes or sports and can occur in a variety of activities, from small and large. Whether you're a mechanic, musician, doctor, electrician, teacher, talk show host, chemist, artist, or even a gardener, you can achieve flow or find yourself in a zone. When increased focus and attention are paired with skills that meet performance requirements, reaching a state of flow or working your way into a zone are more likely to take place. Mr. Csikszentmihalyi's book *Flow: The Psychology of Optimal Experience* provides more extensive science, more vivid anecdotes, and more broad-based research discussing flow in incisive detail.

Why is *flow* pertinent to *Genius? Interest* drives *motivation. Motivation* drives *attention. Attention* drives *action* (our actions). The article *The Science of Attention* emphasizes the significance of attention:

> Paying attention is a task people take for granted; they rarely stop to think about the complex neurocognitive processes involved…. Paying attention is the first step in the learning process….

Without repetitive actions, such as intense study, deliberate practice, and sustained focus, developing a high level of dexterity and facility in any given activity, sport, vocation, career field, or skill can be more challenging. The article goes on:

> In order to efficiently process the huge amounts of information absorbed every second, the brain must impose several control measures. This starts with the prioritization of different types of stimuli, a process that controls what information to ignore and what to recognize and how much concentration to give particular elements.
>
> The brain also connects new information to prior knowledge to aid the understanding of a new piece as well as to develop a clearer idea about broader concepts. Finally, it helps a person to focus attention on important aspects for an appropriate amount of time. The latter can be a difficult task when the subject is not inherently interesting.

It requires more effort to develop your unique Genius (*The Einstein Within*) if you are not interested in the pursuit, goal, or project to which it is being applied. When *The Einstein Within* (your *Einstein Within*) is laser focused on a pursuit that is intrinsically interesting to you, that you are passionate or naturally energized about, achieving flow or climbing your way into a zone is more likely than not to occur. When you are in flow, employing creativity, engaging imagination, making thought connections (whether new or previously discovered), galvanizing the human body to perform optimally (as Jordan did), or cultivating the fruits of *The Einstein Within* occurs much more organically.

As such, the constellation between interest, motivation, focused attention, action, flow (zone), and *The Einstein Within* (Genius) are inextricably linked.

* * * *

Regardless of the perceived level of grandeur associated with a person's given Genius, that person is no more or less worthy of respect and appreciation than you and I. Albert Einstein and Misty Copeland both ventured through their own journey, ultimately becoming standouts in their chosen fields. The people we see and interact with on a day-to-day basis should be seen in the same light and given an equal amount of respect for the uniqueness and Genius they offer; we short change them when we don't. You and I have ventured or are venturing through our own respective journey to share *The Einstein Within* us all.

There is a co-worker of mine who, in my mind, fittingly helps sketch out the remaining takeaways encapsulated within Amendment VI. Up to this point, most of the people used to illustrate ideas throughout this book are names widely known. For anonymity, I will refer to my co-worker as "Bill." Bill is not famous nor is he wealthy. I met Bill sometime in the 2014 to 2015 timeframe. We worked for the same organization at one point, supporting the same projects. If I had to guess, he is approximately 5'10" tall, weighing a modest 185lbs. When in his presence, Bill comes across in a most unassuming, yet energetic way. He is the kind of person who, when you speak with him, you feel as if he tunes everything else out. Engaging in his current conversation is seemingly his only priority. In a world where there is a constant emphasis on being able to multitask, Bill's personality and aura are very refreshing. He not only engages in conversation, but he also does so with noticeable facility, swimmingly volleying his perspectives thoughtfully and insights carefully. I have gathered he pulls from a wide base of experiences accumulated over the years, which make him well versed on a wide variety of topics. He naturally exudes warmth—I don't believe I have ever left a conversation with him not feeling mentally energized.

It does not take very long being in Bill's presence before you see firsthand some of the unique attributes associated with his Einstein Within (Genius). Before you can fully appreciate Bill as a person, it's important to have more context, and learning more about his education helps accomplish just that. For the purposes of this book, I asked Bill several questions regarding his background and also the topic of genius. He attended a Catholic University in Milwaukee, Wisconsin where he received his Bachelor of Arts (BA) in Political Science and Broadcast Communications. He attended college thanks to a 4-year Reserve Officers' Training Corps (ROTC) scholarship. He then matriculated at a Catholic law school in Washington D.C. Bill's favorite classes were Constitutional Law, contracts, and, in his words, any business-related law. Due to his 4-year obligation to the military after finishing law school, Bill went to work in the Judge Advocate General's (JAG) Corps where he did Military Justice in Oklahoma. He would move on to work legal assistance services in Korea before finally being able to obtain his ideal assignment. In his world, in his mind, applying his vast body of knowledge and expertise to Government Contracting in the Pentagon was his ideal assignment. Today, Bill no longer serves in the military; however, he still works as a Government Contracting Legal Attorney for the U.S. Government.

The first time I entered Bill's office I remember seeing framed color photos of each of his eight children, both boys and girls, in a straight line on his bookshelf. A genuinely proud dad who loves his children, Bill is not shy about voicing his profound appreciation for the joy they bring to him and his wife. Before we delved into work related questions, I believe I initially commented on his noticeably large family. By today's standard, eight children are likely considered a rather large family. Bill then pointed to each of them, told me their respective names, and shared a little about each. His eyes lit up when he spoke. By the time we finished discussing his children, it was clear to me the amount of care, thought, diligence he and his wife puts into their responsibility as nurturers. We eventually moved on and covered the work-related topic I had originally stopped by to examine.

Fast forward more than four years later. I visited Bill's office again, needing his valuable insights for another work project. We again began talking about his children. This time around, his eldest son, who we'll call George, was the topic of discussion. George, I found out, enjoys making music. At that time, George, as a member of a larger team, had recently contributed original music for a video game. Bill's elation for George's achievement was etched all over his face. Although usually very measured, his euphoria was obvious as we listened to some of the game's soundtrack his son wrote. Bill was not only excited for his son; he was also conspicuously proud as George's parent. How often can anyone say that I have personally contributed original music for a video game or that I am a parent of someone who has done so.

As a child, my brother, sister, and I loved playing video games. Not only are video games fun, they also can be challenging, exciting to the imagination, and at the most basic level be a very stimulating activity. An arcade game released by Nintendo in 1983, *Mario Bros. (the Mario Brothers)* was the first video game I played. The game revolved around two plumbers, Mario and Luigi, who traverse their way through the sewers of New York. Staving off a variety of enemies, through varying levels of difficulty in phases, the Mario Bros. receive their pay by collecting coins. Eventually, through concentration and focus, my young, elementary level brain at the time finally conquered the entire game. As a kid, that was quite an accomplishment.

Mario Bros. was one of many video games my siblings and I immersed ourselves into. It goes without saying that visuals and graphics are important elements to the overall gaming experience. However, regardless of the video game, the music (i.e., sound effects included) that accompany each phase, level, or round of a given game is also a significant element of the gaming experience. A well-done musical composition can help to produce a magical ride as we navigate the video game terrain. Some games have a way of hypnotizing us, rendering it nearly impossible to relinquish our attention from the virtual world in which we have immersed ourselves for hours on end. The arduous pursuit packaged in progressively measured levels of difficulty combined with the ebbs and flows inherent with a game's storyline can be addictive. We find our pulse rate, our heart beat elevating at various junctures throughout. Sometimes, certain rhythms and chords can trigger an even keener focus or potentially lull us to sleep. Therefore, inserting the right sound, at the most fitting time, to produce the most desirable affect is an art within itself. That is what makes George's musical contribution so significant. Being able to successfully execute that affect requires a certain kind of talent, a certain kind of creativity and imagination, a certain kind of Genius—George's *Einstein Within* is uniquely capable of doing just that.

My intent here is not focusing necessarily on the Genius of George's dad, Bill. Bill's Genius is unique and incredible in its own right. However, George is the focus coupled along with highlighting valuable insights we can glean from a parenting perspective. There is no such thing as "perfection," although the word obviously exits. Furthermore, from a parenting standpoint, to say there is no such thing as "perfection" is an understatement. Regardless of which continent you find yourself, every parent generally wants the best for their child. Different circumstances, whether cultural, level of education, economic and financial conditions, or other dynamics affect the kind of parenting a child receives. Here is the bottom line—there is no perfect remedy or formula to create the perfect environment to mold the perfect child. Parents are human beings. Across the globe, parents use what they know to stitch, knit together an environment conducive for their child to grow, develop, and, hopefully, prosper to the best of their knowledge.

George is the Genius you and I are more likely to encounter in our day-to-day lives. He is not famous. George's name is not included in any *Time 100* or any other magazine's "most influential people" list. Eventually, I had a chance to engage and communicate with George, and here's some of what I learned. He is a very modest and humble person; that was my immediate observation. Arrogant and pompous are adjectives antithetical to his personhood. George has a refreshingly transparent, straight-forward, very sincere style of communication. When speaking with him, you get the impression he has no desire to try and woo anyone; not even a smidgen of pretension.

When I asked him directly, George responded he does not consider himself a genius. Despite, in my mind, his obvious musical talent, he is reluctant to assign to himself the label genius. With his usual demure, he said "I'm too familiar with my ideas to call them anything like that." George, however, does consider Mr. Jacob Collier to be a genius. Having no familiarity with Jacob, I researched him to learn more. Jacob, I discovered, is a versatile artist, who, amongst other talents, possesses a broad range of musical skill as a singer, composer, and multi-instrumentalist. His talents have been recognized to the degree that famous pro-ducer-composer Quincy Jones signed him to his manage-ment company. George further elaborated, "He [Jacob] just has such a command over his music and exceptional ability at playing, writing and comprehending/communicating advanced musical concepts." Here is the irony, I thought, as George shared his appreciation for Jacob Collier. Many times, we see *genius* in others far more clearly, far easier than we can see *Genius* within ourselves.

The more George shared about himself, shared about his Genius, the more fascinated I became. At age 10 or 11, he found out he could record his own multi-track arrangements on his keyboard. George continued:

Before[,] I'd make my own versions of video game tunes I love[,] until I realized with the tools at my disposal[,] I could give my own ideas a life outside my head. I've been writing music in some form ever since. As for wanting to pursue a career in music, I'm very shy. I recognized this put me at a disadvantage for most 'real' jobs[,] but composers seem to do most of their work behind closed doors[,] so it sounded like a good fit for me. But aside from wanting to become more professional about it, just improving myself as a composer and musician brings me a lot of joy and self-satisfaction.

George's intrinsic interest in music became apparent to him in his pre-adolescent years. His unyielding interest in music was initially misunderstood and misinterpreted by his parents, which can happen sometimes. According to George, his parents were convinced he had a "computer addiction." In reality, what his parents misunderstood to be a computer addiction was George's innate passion and interest in music—his mom and dad eventually self-corrected their misunderstanding, developing a parallel appreciation for his individuality, passion, and interest. George was acutely aware of how creating music led to a deep abiding fulfillment no amount of money can buy. Having his personal ideas exist outside his head or outside his internal world, as described by Sir Ken Robinson in *Out of Our Minds: Learning to be Creative*, for other people to enjoy with him is what George specifically enjoys about making music. I asked him, "What experience do you want those hearing your music to feel or experience when they hear your music during the course of playing a particular game?" Here is how George responded:

> As for what I want to convey with music, I want to create a multitude of experiences for people who hear it. Maybe even something surprising here and there.

As of 2020, George has contributed to 1 released video game, but has written for several. His once fledgling Genius continues to expand daily. George is not currently tied to a particular company. He has been doing freelance music work for about 3 years while attending college.

I was curious how well George performed while in school on a subject he did not find interesting. As usual, he was very transparent in his response. In "Writing" for example, George made "Bs" and "Cs." He was used to getting "As" in other subjects. According to George, "….it was discouraging getting bad grades for not learning enough things that I thought were really neat[,] but not exactly memorable." I can personally identify with George. There are certain subjects that simply are not interesting enough to make the mental effort to remember and socialize in my active memory—it is that simple. The root cause has nothing to do with intelligence; it has more to do with interest.

I acknowledge there are some instances when an inability to learn is directly correlated to an individual's lack of comprehension or potentially other reasons; in George's particular experience, this is not the case. It is important to communicate and identify this distinction.

George is a great example of the catalytic effect of attention and the inextricable constellation between interest, motivation, attention, focused action, flow (zone), and *The Einstein Within (Genius)*. Let us *connect the dots (CTD)*. We all have varying levels of interest in different areas. Furthermore, we also excel and require more development in different areas. As I learned more about George's formative years from his dad, his interest and undeniable Genius to compose music make sense. Bill added, "[W]hen he is in the creative zone[,] it is difficult to get him to do anything else to include schoolwork, chores, etc." Although George finds the mechanics of translating his thoughts into words on paper arduous, he has the ability; however, he finds the subject uninteresting, is dispassionate about doing it, does not put forth the mental discipline to perform it well consistently, and, as a consequence, made Bs and Cs in this area throughout his school years.

I asked Bill whether he considered George a genius. In addition, he provided further insight into the origin of his son's interest in music. I found his response and insight refreshing and very encouraging. Bill answered my question this way:

> I would say that [George] is a musical genius. The way he will work for hours to figure out how to extract a

certain sound or sound blend from the various music composing programs he uses to compose his music I think is genius. He has in his head what he wants the sound to be[,] then he works for hours trying to figure out how to make the sound happen with the programs he works with.

Bill shared more:

> [George] has perfect pitch[,] which was a real problem when he was young and we'd be at church and someone behind him would sing off key. He would either hold his ears or hide under the pew to avoid the off-key singing. We had an old piano from my wife's grandfather.... His grandmother bought him an electronic keyboard when he was five and he taught himself to play piano in short order. We noticed when he was about seven or eight that he started to compose his own music.

Perfect pitch defined is "the ability to recognize the pitch of a note or produce any given note." George was born with perfect pitch; that inherent trait added to his Genius and his ability to synthesize music notes, process clusters of various sounds, disentangle unsavory melodies, and compose music of his own that represents his unique creativity. If perfect pitch was not one of his many traits, it would not necessarily mean George would not have a similar interest in or ear for music. His perfect pitch sensitivity simply creates a distinct ripple in his mind, in his internal world that contributes to the unique Genius he has to offer to musical composition or any other creative, mental, or physical pursuit he chooses to partake. Every trait, characteristic, or attribute that George has, that we have, that *Everyone* has, encompasses a *Unique Genius Profile Composite (UGPC)*; it is up to each of us to endeavor how best to maximize it (not exploit it).

Before asking my previous question about George's genius, I was not exactly sure how Bill would answer. In my experience, people tend to be less inclined to perceive themselves or those they know to be "geniuses." To my pleasant surprise, Bill not only responded in the affirmative that George is a musical genius, he also indicated "several" of his other seven children are geniuses in their own way. Bill also has a son who has "really bad attention-deficit/ hyperactivity disorder (ADHD)." However, Bill explained, "the connections that he makes between different things [are] amazing at times (when he can focus)."

I wondered, as parents, did Bill and his wife have a specific approach/philosophy to developing/educating George and his other siblings from the outset or was their approach more akin to attempting to be thoughtful parents and provide the best advice/parenting they knew how? So, I decided to ask Bill that question directly, and here is some of what I learned. Bill and his wife decided early on to home school their children. He emphasized each of his children has their own unique learning style and that each child is completely different from one another. He further noted, "[w]hat may have worked with one child doesn't work or is counterproductive for another child." Some are completely self-motivated and self-taught, and others learn from reading. Another learns more by talking with Bill's wife about subjects. In their estimation, this enables the classroom to follow her (and him) in the car. Others work well on the computer and web based educational techniques while a couple get completely distracted by being on the computer and will default into searches of things they want to look up rather than what they are supposed to be working on. Some of his other children are more hands on. His wife also believes in reading aloud to the children and sets time aside to do that. Bill's teenage daughter has now taken to reading a bed time chapter to her little sisters.

With respect to home schooling, although used in Bill's case, I understand that it is not an option available to everyone. The level of awareness and understanding Bill and his wife have developed over the years for each of their children's learning style are of chief importance and my focus here. Their awareness and understanding have grown as their time spent with and intentional attention to each of their children have expanded. They have used what they have learned to tailor a favorable environment that is conducive for each of their children to explore, discover, develop, chisel, and maximize their respective infinite potential. Bill and his wife are not wealthy. They are a modest middle-class family. With eight children, they wish more money and resources were available to provide more opportunities for them. For example, in George's case, technology and affordability limitations have restricted Bill and his wife's ability to get the latest and greatest music composing technologies. However, they believe "in some ways[,] the lack of resources forced him [George] to think about how to extract as much out of the programs and technology he had available." Bill underscored, "[it] forced him [George] to think creatively."

In my humble opinion, as a parent and nurturer, Bill represents a parent with a healthy perspective. I am not a child psychologist, nor do I have a PhD on how to raise children and be an effective parent—these are simply my views. *All* (not only *"several"*) of his other seven children are *Geniuses* in their own way. As we have learned throughout the pages of this book, *Everyone is an Einstein; and There is an Einstein in Everyone.* I have not met or communicated with Bill's remaining seven children; however, just as in George's case, each of them has traits and interests that make them unique. Similar to George, similar to Albert Einstein, each of them, each of you have a *Unique Genius Profile Composite (UGPC).* Bill's remaining children, I suspect, are on their own journey of evolving their respective Genius, similar to you and I. The Einstein, the Genius in Everyone needs only to be developed, cultivated, harnessed, and honed. George discovered music is an area he is organically drawn to, and as such, has poured his time, energy, and imagination into the evolution of his Genius over the years. George's Genius is extraordinary, undeniable, unique, elastic, and a non-stationary-force that resides in him and is continually being developed throughout his life.

George's most pronounced Genius applies to musical composition. Like Misty Copeland, Jim Carrey, Christopher Langan, Albert Einstein, you, me, *Everyone,* George's Genius was in its incubation period when he was a child. Through dedicated effort and intentional development, his Genius has matured, evolved over the years. Again, he has the ability to apply his Genius to any other arena if he so chooses. I asked George what would be his dream career? He shared being a composer at Nintendo (Nintendo Co., Ltd.) is his dream. Nintendo is a Japanese electronics and video game company; it is also the gaming system brand I first received as a kid. My Nintendo system came with the first video game I ever played. The video game I'm referring to is Mario Bros. George will not become a Genius after maybe becoming a composer at Nintendo one day. In addition, he does not need to win the Nobel Prize or similar award or receive worldwide recognition to be considered a Genius. George was born a Genius!

AFTERWORD

Genius

Only you can bring our world the *Genius* (*The Einstein Within*) that exits in your mind, in your internal world. The potential that resides in each of us is infinite. Our respective story and journey are different and similar at the same time. No story and journey are exactly the same and beauty permeates them all. Despite past and current conditions, very chaotic and maybe uncomfortable environments, become a *Pathfinder* and make a way for your Genius if necessary. As I learned from *Failing Forward* by John C. Maxwell, there is no such thing as failure or a mistake if you choose to perceive them as "learning opportunities." Your perception, our perception is key. Fully embrace each "learning opportunity" that surfaces throughout your journey to refine your Genius.

Through *Everyone is an Einstein; and There is an Einstein in Everyone: The Constitution of Genius*, I encourage you, I encourage Everyone to "take the leap and build your wings," build your Genius and share it with us in whatever form it comes. Remember that *comfort* (being comfortable) in just about any endeavor or pursuit where our *attention* is focused breeds *confidence*. *Confidence* coupled with *intentional practice* and *repetition* can breed *grace, command*, and ultimately *proficiency*. Furthermore, *interest* is the metaphorical motor that drives *motivation*. *Motivation* adds gas to fuel *focused attention*. *Focused attention* is the electrical power source that accelerates *action* (our action), which can potentially ignite *flow* (the *"zone"*) where *Genius* is in its most kinetic state; where *your Genius* is in its most kinetic state. There is *endless value* in now having this *heightened awareness* to undergird the way we understand ourselves and each other.

I see a near future where a deeper level of appreciation, a more robust feeling of compassion, and a stronger sense of empathy exists for the *Genius Everyone offers,* regardless of its stage on the development spectrum. In that future, we are not narrowly self-focused. We (all of us) are also people-focused and centered. *Everyone is a Genius* and should know and believe that, approaching each day of life with that ever-present awareness. It is not narcissistic to confidently carry that inner awareness with us everywhere we go. When *Genius* is understood and carried with *humility, individually* and *collectively, we can accomplish amazing feats!*

References

Begley, S. (2007). *Train Your Mind Change Your Brain: How a New Science Reveals Our Extraordinary Potential to Transform Ourselves.* New York, NY: The Random House Publishing Group.

Biography (2014). *Natalie Portman Biography.* Retrieved from Biography Online http://www.biography.com/people/natalie-portman-9542326#synopsis

Copeland, M. (2014). *Life in Motion: An Unlikely Ballerina.* New York, NY: Touchstone.

Dodson, A. (2017). *On This Day in NBA Finals History: Michael Jordan's 'Shrug Game'.* Retrieved from The Undefeated Online. https://theundefeated.com/features/nba-finals-history-michael-jordan-shrug-game/

Doidge M.D., N. (2007). *The Brain that Changes Itself: Stories of Personal Triumph from the Frontiers of Brain Science.* New York, NY: Penguin Group (USA).

Geography Education National Implementation Project (GENIP). *Geography Standard 11: The Patterns and Networks of Economic Interdependence on Earth's Surface.* Accessed 29 February 2020. https://www.nationalgeographic.org/standards/national-geography-standards/11/

Geography Education National Implementation Project (GENIP). *National Geography Standards Index "Geography is for Life in Every Sense of That Expression: Lifelong, Life-Sustaining, and Life-Enhancing."* Accessed 29 February

2020. https://www.nationalgeographic.org/standards/national-geography-standards/

Gladwell, M. (2011). *Outliers: The Story of Success.* New York, NY: Back Bay Books / Little, Brown and Company Hachette Book Group.

Gutierrez, K. (2014). *The Science of Attention (And Why eLearning Professionals Should Care).* Retrieved from Shift Disruptive eLearning Online. https://www.shiftelearning.com/blog/bid/349806/the-science-of-attention-and-why-elearning-professionals-should-care

His Holiness The Dalai Lama, & Cutler, H. (2009). *The Art of Happiness in a Troubled World.* New York, NY: Little, Crown Publishing Group.

History.com Editors (February 21, 2020). *Constitution.* Retrieved from History Online. https://www.history.com/topics/united-states-constitution/constitution

Isaacson, W. (2007). *Einstein.* New York, NY: Simon & Schuster.

Jutze (2014). *The Natalie Portman Story.* Retrieved from Natalie Portman Online. http://www.natalieportman.com/?page_id=108

It's a Wonderful Life (1946) – Awards (2014). Retrieved from Imdb Online. http://www.imdb.com/title/tt0038650/awards

It's a Wonderful Life (1946) – Full cast and crew (2014). Retrieved from Imdb Online. http://www.imdb.com/title/tt0038650/fullcredits

Lewis, J. (2016). *Jazz Prodigy Jacob Collier: 'Quincy Jones Told Me Jazz is the Classical Music of Pop'.* Retrieved from The Guardian Online. https://www.theguardian.com/music/2016/

jul/07/jazz-prodigy-jacob-collier-i-knew-the-sounds-i-wanted-i-just-had-to-find-out-how-to-make-them

Maxwell, J. (2007). *Talent is Never Enough: Discover the Choices That Will Take You Beyond Your Talent.* Nashville, TN: Thomas Nelson, Inc.

Noland, C. (2014). *Child Actor Played Early George Bailey.* Retrieved from LA Times Online. http://articles.latimes.com/2008/jun/08/local/me-anderson8

Phillips, C. (2016). *Breaking Barriers on Stage: African American Ballet Dancers Who Made History.* Retrieved from PBS Online. http://www.pbs.org/independentlens/blog/breaking-barriers-on-the-stage-african-american-ballet-dancers-history/

Rattini, K. B. (2019). *General Hannibal Was One of the Most Creative Military Strategists in History.* Retrieved from National Geographic Online. https://www.nationalgeographic.com/culture/people/reference/hannibal/

Robert J. Anderson (2014). Retrieved from Imdb Online. http://www.imdb.com/name/nm0026434/

Robert J. Anderson – Biography (2014). Retrieved from Imdb Online. http://www.imdb.com/name/nm0026434/bio?ref_=nm_ql_1

Robinson, K. (2011). *Out of Our Minds: Learning to be Creative.* Chichester, West Sussex, United Kingdom: Capstone Publishing Ltd. (A Wiley Company).

Worthington, V. *Being in the Zone: The Flow State in Athletic Endeavors.* Accessed 7 March 2020. https://breakingmuscle.com/fitness/being-in-the-zone-the-flow-state-in-athletic-endeavors

Acknowledgements

This book is written in memoriam to my dear mom. My work ethic is a reflection of her *relentless* spirit. Her purity of heart and kindness are hallmarks of what made her so special. My dad's vision and tenacity were intrinsic attributes that made him unique. Both my mom and dad provided fertile foundation for my siblings and I to thrive. I thank my brother and sister for their support and encouragement over the years.

On July 16, 2012, I began the journey of writing this book. I am so profoundly excited to finally share it with the world. I would like to extend my sincerest gratitude to Malcolm Gladwell and Sir Ken Robinson—the books you have written inspired me.

I am fortunate to have great friends who generously offered their time and insights to help shape this book. Each of you have my heartfelt thanks:

To Susan Julian, whom I have known since 2007, your thoughtful insights and manuscript reviews were always spot on.

Countless thanks to The Smith Family: Phil, Anne, Emily, Josh, and Willa—your loving family is a shining example of grace. Every human being should have a friend with such boundless wisdom and who is as dependable as you Phil.

To my dear friend Darren Baker, your thought-provoking feedback throughout helped tremendously. I certainly benefited from your wise counsel.

I doubt that I can properly capture in words how grateful I am to Khalilah Thomas. She is a phenomenal thinker in her own right. Infinite thanks for lending your Genius to the overall process and manuscript reviews.

To Christopher and Melissa Barrett, thanks again for your preliminary thoughts at the outset.

I would be remiss if I did not extend my utter gratitude to Candice Dow. Your encouragement helped lay the groundwork to begin this book.

My sincerest thanks and appreciation to Bill and George for your candor and willingness to share your story in Amendment VI.

Lastly, many thanks to a few longtime friends of mine: Nick, Roland, Kevin, John, and Damian. The relationships and friendships I have with each of you are also sources of inspiration.

I am imbued with intrigue and wonder for life and all of its simplicity, complexity, and everything in between. That intrigue and wonder led me to pen this book—I genuinely hope it inspires *Everyone* to share *your Genius*.

Index